HOW
RELEVANT
IS THE
BIBLE?

and other commentaries on scripture

HOW
RELEVANT
IS THE
BIBLE?

and other commentaries on scripture

by

JOHN L. McKENZIE

THE THOMAS MORE PRESS
Chicago, Illinois

Some of the material in this book has appeared
in previously printed or recorded format.

ISBN 0-88347-125-6

Contents

How Relevant Is the Bible?
7

The Real Jesus
27

The Real Mary
43

Myths in the Bible
63

The Book of Revelation
83

The Book of Job
95

Isaiah
119

War and Peace in the New Testament
137

Evaluating the Deluge Myth
151

The State in Christian Perspective
165

The Bible: A Progress Report
187

How Relevant Is the Bible?

I AM told that wide popular interest in the Bible has not flagged, that people still go back to the Bible for something that they do not feel they can get elsewhere. I have to ask myself whether this is validated by my own experience and the experience of colleagues. The fact that biblical courses are proliferating all over secular campuses does not really validate what I am told. This shows that young people are still discovering the Bible. What I hear is that older people are still cherishing it.

So I come back to the question why people return to the Bible. It certainly is not from a rewarding search for doctrine. More than a few of us have been saying so long that the Bible does not contain a package of doctrine, that it can even be embarrassing to those who try to prepare a package of doctrine, that we seem to have removed this as a motive for biblical studies. We have been suspected of hostility to doctrinal formulations and systems, not without some foundation, and of hinting broadly that the search for truth is better than its possession. This is not a charge which I would wish to disclaim entirely. We have learned, perhaps not early enough, that security in the possession of truth can be based upon delusion. Consider the once secure possession of the truth that the world is flat. Consider the anger aroused when this security was challenged. Consider that it was not merely a single erroneous belief that was challenged, there was challenged also a whole approach to man's understanding of nature and man's understanding of the Bible. We have still not dealt thoroughly and finally with these challenges.

The entire discussion of biblical and scientific astronomy and cosmology was a part of the struggle to establish the validity of enquiry or, to use the words I used earlier, the validity of the search for truth on the principle that man never knows it all about anything. If there is such a thing as a modern mind, this refusal to claim comprehension is one of the principles by which it works. We accept it in other human activities. Theology seems to be the last area of thought in which it will be accepted. Possibly people return to the Bible because they sense that biblical studies are in harmony with the mentality which they know and live with in politics, business and industry, the mentality which always refuses to take the existing methods as ultimate, the existing information as irreformable. There may be something demonic about western man's insatiable quest for knowledge, generally because he believes that knowedge will show him a better way to do it. But this is the mind to which the church must address itself and it is a mind which will not listen to a statement that there is nothing to learn. The Bible does not so much give answers as lead to answers. It puts the right questions directly in a form which does not permit evasion. It confronts us with challenges to action which are urgent. Some examples may illustrate what I mean.

In a world in which war is no longer the sport of kings but a threat, many think, to human survival itself, the issues of war and peace have become matters of wide popular concern, especially in societies which are, or pretend to be, democratic. It has become obvious even to the most confirmed secularist that these issues are moral as well as political. If war is too important to be left to the generals, it is also too important to be left to the politicians. It takes no more than a superficial reading of the New Testament to see that war is not mentioned among the solutions of basic human problems. Hence the inevitable question is why Jesus ignored something which most of mankind for most of human history has made a primary interest. What do we need which war achieves? If Jesus does not include this among our basic needs, should we not reconsider our needs if we take him seriously? It is not merely an element of the New Testament but also the Old Testament.

As I have mentioned, I do not wish to speak of biblical doctrine but rather of questions. In most of the books of the Old Testament, war is taken for granted as part of the human condition. Yet some of the prophets, when they addressed the people of Israel and Judah, not only deny that war is a legitimate means of self defense, they affirm that it is a sin against the justice of God. It is, I think, a safe paraphrase of their words to say that the people whom they address are denied the moral power and authority to conduct war, that no one is good enough to conduct war.

This, I submit, raises questions rather than answers them. And among the questions must be a moral self-examination on a national scale, and an examination of what might be a moral base for conducting war. Possibly we might discover that there is no moral base. We might have to go beyond venerating Jesus as the man of peace who sets up impossible moral ideals. We venerate him while declaring him irrelevant to decisions of public policy. This scarcely establishes a Christian community. When the issues of war and peace arise, one's mind is led into the further consideration of the doubtful fruits of violence in society. We usually do not reflect on how much of our social fabric is sustained by violence. Like war, it is a part of our society because we feel compelled to do it. Whatever one may say about the exaggeration of nonresistance, it seems clear that Jesus in no way accepted violence as a means of controlling violence. This is not to establish an absolute, as some have said. It does establish a moral direction in which the Christian individual and the Christian community must move if they are to remain Christian. It is visionary to pretend that such a moral transformation is easy or quick. If I may quote myself, I have said that the church has never accepted adultery as a part of normal living, but I do not think it has ever realistically expected to abolish it. It is a struggle which the church never wins but never quite loses either. So, likewise, one does not restrain violence by conceding its necessity.

The attitude one takes towards these questions discloses another question which the Bible imposes upon us and it may be put this way: why have Christians so often felt that they are excused from doing what they know is right until everyone else has done it first? The New Testament seems to assume that they who hear the word will do it without waiting for social pressure. Indeed, they will create social pressure. To illustrate by returning to the question of war and violence, men always assume that there is a security in violence and a risk in peacemaking. Surely experience has validated the gospel aphorism that they who take the sword perish by the sword. It is a part of the human condition that men will take risks doing what they know is wrong which they will not take doing what is right. The gospel compels us to ask ourselves why we live this way. The topics of wealth and poverty are mentioned in the gospels perhaps as often as any other single topics. The questions raised by the New Testament have never been answered by Christians. The words were uttered in a world with a different social and economic structure from the world of western Christianity.

In the Hellenistic Roman world, most of the wealth was concentrated in a very few hands. The vast majority of people lived in near destitution which did not permit them literally to be sure of where they would get their food for the next day. This kind of marginal existence is familiar in most of the countries of the world but not in the middle-class countries in which the Christian churches have their strength. This implies that most of the world outside the Christian west lives in conditions identical with those in which the Gospel words were uttered. It seems to imply also that the Christian world has produced conditions to which the Gospel words are not directly addressed. There are dangers implicit in such reservations. Again, it seems, we find that the Bible does not deliver doctrine which we can easily apply to our situation. The words of Jesus on wealth and poverty do continue the words of the Old Testament prophets who speak with severity about those who oppress the poor and the helpless.

God is not partial, as the Old Testament books remark more than once. But if he shows anything that looks like partiality, it is shown on behalf of those who are powerless and have no powerful friends. The Old Testament words are of a piece with the blessings which Jesus declares upon the poor and the helpless, blessings which, in the gospel of Luke, are matched with woes upon the rich and the powerful. The thrust of the sayings is without doubt that he who has acquired much wealth is probably a scoundrel. Again, it is Luke who has preserved a saying in which the wealthy landowner is addressed as, "You fool, tonight your life will be demanded." These words seem harsh to the modern Christian because he lives in a society which has successfully distributed more wealth to more people than any other society known to history. He may feel that in a society where poverty is defined by the possession of black-and-white TV against color TV, the gospel words are hardly relevant.

If the words of the gospel can be summarized in some principles, one such principle would certainly be that no one should enjoy the luxuries of life while another is deprived of the necessities. The words of the gospel seem to imply that the wealthy, like the poor, will always be with us and the wealthy should always share of their abundance with those who have basic unfulfilled needs. Paul, a respected interpreter of the gospel, did not say that all should become equally impoverished. He said that those who have more should give to those who have less until a certain equality arises.

This, in line with what I have been pursuing, is a question rather than an answer. This does not yet touch an implication in the words of the gospels that the desire for wealth and not merely its possession is, in the words of one of the epistles, the root of evil. It does appear that we preserve this gospel saying in a somewhat modified form, making distinctions between the legitimate acquisition of wealth and the illegitimate. This is indeed an attempt to answer the unspoken question in the gospel principle. It seemed to suggest that as long as the acquisition meets the standards of legitimacy established by the society, one need feel no concern. In Luke's parable of the rich man who dines sumptuously each day while the poor man starved at his door, the rich man is not called a thief. To risk repetition, he poses a question to which Jesus, as he is quoted, gave no answer except sell what you have and give to the poor. This may be an example of exaggeration like plucking out the eye that scandalizes you. But neither saying recommends doing nothing different from what you have been doing.

It may be risky to suggest that the words of the gospel do not imply that avarice is a vice into which only the wealthy can fall. Or that the equality desired by Paul is to be achieved by plundering the haves. The gospel really never offers anything but free choices of alternatives. If one does what is right, it is not right if one does it under compulsion.

Some liberation theologians have found the gospel irrelevant to modern times because it is addressed to the individual person rather than to society. They seem to imply that society and not persons should be changed, or rather, that the persons will be changed if the society is changed. There seems to be a clear opposition here between the biblical approach to human problems and most modern approaches which can be summed up not unfairly as political. The modern ideal is the change by reformation or by revolution of institutions. Once the institutions are regenerated, men will do what they ought by institutional compulsion. And the institutions will determine what they ought to do.

I said earlier that the gospel offers nothing but free choices of alternatives. Institutional compulsion removes free choice as far as possible and exerts all possible pressure on the individual to accept a choice which has already been made for him. A feature of the Book of Jeremiah which has not always been noticed is that Jeremiah announces the total end of all religious, political and social institutions of the society in which he lived. More is said here than what many readers think are conventional announcements of doom in the biblical prophets. The threats of Jeremiah are directed against specific institutions by name. He announces an institutional vacuum. In whatever visions of the future may be attributed to Jeremiah, nothing arises to replace the institutions. No king, no temple, no priesthood, no law, no teaching. God will deal with each individual directly. There is no more unambiguous declaration of a lack of faith in human institutions in the entire Bible. Jeremiah does not expect the Israelite institutions which failed so totally to be reestablished.

We are seeking questions, not doctrine, and the question which Jeremiah raises is the question of the competence of institutions. No doubt Jeremiah overstates his case. The Bible often does that. Such an anti-institutional stance which verges upon anarchy will be thought an overstatement by any reader once its import is grasped. Jeremiah, for instance, does not see any religious institutions in his future. If we seek questions, we may be moved to ask whether we expect more from religious institutions than they can deliver. This is not meant to imply that they deliver nothing. I mention religious institutions because in the minds of most church members they have a special status. At the same time, I am not sure that even church members think their religious institutions are agents of salvation as effective as their political institutions.

If I read the minds of my contemporaries aright, they expect the reign of sin and death to be repelled by their political institutions more than by the church. They do put their trust in princes. Why does the New Testament, like the prophets, speak of a change of heart and not a reform of institutions? One may adduce that the primitive church was a church of the poor and the helpless, of the politically powerless. To change the Roman empire was to them as practical a prospect as to change the climate. The fact remains that eventually Christianity did change the Roman empire, even though the cost of making the empire Christian was that the church became Roman. That price it now appears need not have been paid.

It is true that primitive Christians were politically powerless. It is also true that a way of belief and a way of life emerged which could be sustained independently of political institutions. I was impressed when I observed, on my first visit to what is called missionary territory, that it was generally assumed that the natives, forgive the word, could not become Christian unless they became Europeans first. One is reminded of a saying that early Christians were pacifists for three hundred years until they obtained control of the Roman legions. At the risk of oversimplifying, let me put the antithesis crudely. The Bible is directed to the redemption and regeneration of individual persons. Unless this is accomplished, institutional changes are meaningless. The Bible accepts the popular saying that no system is any better than the people in it. The modern approach seeks to reform the institutions and to achieve the regeneration of the persons through institutional compulsion.

I do not see how both views can be sustained at once. I do not wish to go all the way with Jeremiah on the moral bankruptcy of institutions, although at times it is tempting. One must remember that the organized works of mercy, such as the assistance of the needy with food, clothing and housing, the care of the sick, poor and the aged, the education of the children of the poor and similar activities, did not exist until Christians began them. They are legacies of the church to the modern states and one may observe that they are open to criticism precisely because they are so often impersonal. Financial or tax support is not personal engagement but it is better than nothing. I am probably to be counted among those who refuse Christian absolutes. I have said that Jesus did not annul the law of Judaism to replace it with another law which would do the same thing, only better. But even those who refuse absolutes must admit that Jesus or one of his earlier interpreters reduced the whole system of moral obligation to the love of God above all things and of the neighbor as oneself.

The ultimate question of all which the Bible raises is whether the love of one's neighbor is a viable way of life. Jesus was quite aware of the problems of distributing one's love as the heavenly father distributes rain. That figure is attributed to him. He was quite aware of the problem of conflicting claims of love; for he is said to have quoted a paraphrase of the law which directed Jews to love their neighbor and to hate their enemies. This paraphrase of the law is no more than a capsule description of the relations of man with man from the dawn of history. One may say that it has been sufficiently tested and practiced, for instance, to be measured with some accuracy. From a speculative moral point of view, it may be defensible, for many defend it. As the direction for a way of

John L. McKenzie

life, it is more often intolerable than anything else. Perhaps in no other human activity can we see the character of the individual so clearly exhibited in society. As we have noticed, the primitive church did not speak to the politically powerful.

When Jesus blessed the peacemakers and made reconciliation prior to worship, the words were not addressed to statesmen and to public figures. Where does peace begin? We still do not seem to know. The gospels tell us that it begins with the individual peacemaker. I remember a public discussion in which I used the word reconciliation with reference to some public disputes. A noted civil rights activist who was present observed that his group was ready to reconcile as soon as they got what they wanted. I had never heard what reconciliation is *not* defined so well and so briefly. When people are assured that they are right and that justice is all on their side, they are unwilling to yield, and compromise seems to them to be a covenant with death and a league with hell. They cannot be forgiven for they have done nothing wrong and they cannot forgive for it would be a compromise with evil. These are all reasons why the love of the neighbor and in particular that love which denies to others the right to be my enemy does not seem to be a viable way of life.

Again, we are given to ask questions and the

question here is the validity of the principle which is summed up as the love of one's neighbor and the hatred of one's enemy. I observe that we know the practical worth of this principle very well. Dare we question its basis in moral principles? To paraphrase the gospels, it is little or nothing to reconcile and ask forgiveness when we know we are wrong. Apparently it does not count in the gospels unless we do it when we know we are right. One who pays his debts has given nothing to anyone.

This may lead us to another phrasing of the ultimate question, the question of what Jesus demands. From the beginnings of the church, Christians have understood this to mean everything. Not in the sense that everything may be actually demanded but that nothing is safe, so to speak. Few Christians are asked to yield their life to preserve their Christian commitment. Many are asked to yield to their neighbor in a controversy in which both parties are absolutely sure they are right. We are not asked to yield our life but our self-assurance. This makes peace more effectively than dying. One phrase attributed to Jesus demands more than impoverishment. The denial of self is demanded and this may be paraphrased by the denial that one is anybody. When Paul spoke of putting off the old man of sin to put on Christ, was he saying anything different? It is amazing that Christians have so often used these words to designate the temporary renunciation of tobacco or candy. These are easier to renounce than enmity. Even the powerless can afford the luxury of hating.

Once one recognizes that Jesus utters total demands, one is led then to questions of values, specifically, what is worth dying for? No one can escape death nor may one kill oneself. But the human experience does present situations in which one may save one's life or prolong it by doing something or by not doing something which it lies within one's free choice to do or not to do. It seems the Christian must recognize that there are actions or omissions which would save his life which rational ethics would permit but which the Christian commitment does not allow. At times there may be no Christian way to survive. It goes without question that no decision one could make would be more serious and I believe no one can make if for another. We venerate the martyrs but it is hard to think of any martyr of record who could not have escaped death by doing something which the ethics of reason and nature would tolerate.

This most crucial of all decisions is, as we have observed, not imposed upon most Christians, even though we must consider that a number of people have faced it without recognizing it. If this happened, we must consider that they effectively denied their Christian commitment and ceased to be authentic Christians, even though they retained the name and the church affiliation. It is more likely that the Christian may be faced with the choice of physical danger less than death or loss of material resources, perhaps substantial, which can be avoided only be refusing to fulfill his Christian commitment. One must ask not only what is worth dying for but what is worth the risk of possibly crippling injury or impoverishment. One notices that such decisions must often be made with no time for deliberation and that people respond according to deliberations already made and according to principles already formed and accepted.

Another question, perhaps more important, can be answered with time for deliberation with no implication that it is not urgent. If we are not confronted with the decision about what is worth dying for, we certainly must decide what is worth living for, what deserves the dedication of all that we are and have learned and can do. Few, I suppose, would care to admit that they are dedicated to the acquisition of wealth, even though their life shows no other clear purpose. They would surely say that their dedication is to their family. The family may be an extension of the self. If it is, a profession of family dedication is not entirely candid. One may profess dedication to one's business or profession as an activity by which human needs are met and human suffering alleviated. Again, each one must judge the sincerity of this dedication. But such professions are at least a recognition of the indecency of being dedicated to oneself or only to one's family which, after all, does present a rather limited horizon.

I think of myself as being dedicated to learning, which sounds noble enough. It has not yet demanded renunciation like that which the nation demands of the soldier. If one enjoys doing what one can do, one is indeed fortunate if the pleasurable activity is also remunerative. But one wonders whether the word dedication may not be a flattering word for what one is doing.

Jesus invites one to a dedication to God in one's fellowmen and he assures us that we cannot reach God by bypassing our fellowmen. This demand, which we said is total, sets no age limit at beginning or end, nor minimum degree of wealth or social position or education. It can be achieved by the poor and the powerless to whom the gospel was first proclaimed. It does seem that when the gospel is presented to those who have power, wealth and social position, it loses some of its urgency because such people have so many other ways of self-fulfillment. If one has power or wealth or talent, one sees how much one can do with these things that cannot be done

How Relevant Is the Bible?

without them. Do we who are in this situation see ourselves as reenacting the temptations of Jesus in which wealth, display and power precisely were renounced as means to accomplish his mission? In the world of man it is unnecessary to explain one's dedication to wealth, position and power. They justify themselves. But if one is committed to a belief that these are not supreme values, a word which we reserve for God, we have to ask ourselves how much room this leaves for maneuver between the claims of the world and the challenge of Jesus.

It would be pleasant to conclude that we have in the church the secure guidance which we need to answer these questions. I spoke earlier of the fallacy of expecting institutions to substitute for personal responsibility. To most of the questions I have raised or implied, the church has given no answer which can be turned into a personal choice. Karl Rahner once said that in the most important moral decisions which a person faces in the course of a normal life, he has no explicit directions from his moral teachers. It is good that he does not. It would not only not be the person's own decision, there would be an excellent chance that it would be the wrong decision. Let the Christian accept as gracefully as he can the freedom which Christ has given him.

The Real Jesus

SEVERAL hundred years of Christian art have created a picture of Jesus which has become standard enough to be easily recognized. This picture is entirely the work of the artist's imagination and has no relation to the real historical Jesus.

This conventional picture in fact represents a young adult male of one of the countries from which the artist came, therefore, most frequently, Italian, German, French, Flemish or Spanish. The picture bears no resemblance to a Palestinian villager and we can be sure that it does not resemble a Palestinian villager of the first century of our era.

Our search for the real Jesus begins with the admission that we do not know what he looked like. There is much more we do not know about Jesus. Very few people visit a modern Palestinian village for much longer than it takes to drive through the village. It takes only a brief stop to realize that one is in a new and quite strange world. If Jesus were to enter this world he would be much more at home than we are in the village, and much more at home in the village than he would be with us. I do not mean that the villagers would understand Jesus or the gospel immediately, but they would recognize immediately that he is one of themselves.

We are not certain even of some vital statistics. We know exactly neither the date of his birth nor the date of his death. He was born about the beginning of our era which is incorrectly reckoned from what was thought to be the year of his birth and died about 30 to 35 years later. He was called Jesus of Nazareth because he spent most of his life in Nazareth. Both Matthew and Luke place his birth in Bethlehem. It is my duty to point out that the story of the birth of Jesus in Bethlehem raises a number of serious questions to which no answers have been found. We think we can explain why the birth at Bethlehem was invented. We cannot explain why, if it was not invented, it is mentioned only in the infancy gospels of Matthew and Luke. We know the names of the parents of Jesus and that is all we know about them. Even if the two genealogies of Jesus in the gospels of Matthew and Luke could be verified, and they cannot, we would still know nothing about Joseph and Mary except their names. Joseph appears as more than a name only in the infancy gospel of Matthew. Mary appears as more than a name only in the infancy gospel of Luke.

The Real Jesus

The early years of the lives of most famous men are unknown unless they were the children of famous families. The childhood of Abraham Lincoln is almost totally unknown. It is not surprising that the apocryphal gospels of early Christian centuries were filled with clearly imaginative legends about the birth, infancy and boyhood of Jesus, periods of his life about which the canonical gospels have almost nothing to say. The canonical gospels left ample room for the devout imagination to roam in the early years of the life of Jesus. The biographer in search of Jesus would be grateful for any details about Palestinian village life of the first century or about the parents and kin of Jesus. Such details would add depth and realism to the picture into which we could insert Jesus. At the same time, the biographer would know that Jesus was more than the product of his family and culture. People who achieve distinction in anything are never routine products of their background. Members of the family and culture of distinguished persons are often resentful of the success of those who rise above the expected average. Jesus himself quoted a proverb about the prophet who is recognized everywhere except in his own country. The proverb is quoted in an anecdote about the refusal of the Nazarenes to accept Jesus as anything but the village carpenter. Mark tells us that Jesus' own people thought he was out of his mind and wished to put him under restraint.

Who were his own people? They can hardly be anyone but relatives and friends. Quite clearly they thought that they knew the real Jesus. Quite clearly, they did not. Scholars have engaged in the pursuit of the real Jesus, or the historical Jesus, for well over a hundred years. The search is much less active in contemporary scholarship, not because scholars think they have found the real Jesus but because they think he cannot be found. The gospels, they are sure, present not the real Jesus of history but the Christ of faith. The Christ of faith as a real historical person who was an object of experience to his fellow human beings is, they think, simply not credible.

The real Jesus walked and talked with his fellowmen, lived, suffered and died like them. The Christ of faith was the preexistent son of God who will return in glory on the clouds to judge the living and the dead. The disciples believed that the Jesus whom they knew was identical with the glorious son of God. But they did not experience this identity. Scholars who sought the real historical Jesus believed that by recovering the simple Palestinian villager they might disclose a figure who was historically credible. What is one to make of the transformation of other historical figures such as

The Real Jesus

George Washington and Abraham Lincoln? These men are not remembered as the Virginia planter and the small-town lawyer. They were more than these simple descriptions. And to think of them as no more than such falsifies history. They are remembered for achievements which actually occurred only during a very few years of their lives. The great brooding figure of the Lincoln Memorial statue is not the historical Lincoln. Yet his stature demands such a symbol of the greatness which he achieved. Without the symbol, one has not grasped the real Lincoln.

To say of another that I knew him when he wasn't anybody does not guarantee that one knew him when he became somebody. This is to say that one who refuses the Christ of faith makes it impossible for himself to grasp the real Jesus. Scholars of nearly every shade of belief now accept that Jesus did not present himself as a preexistent son of God who announced that he would come in glory on the clouds to judge the living and the dead, and that those who knew him did not apprehend him as such. These dimensions were attached to Jesus by those who believed in him as Lord and Savior and they were attached to him in the earliest stages of Christianity.

To appeal again to my comparison, they are not unlike the transfiguration of Lincoln which one can witness in the Lincoln Memorial. Does this not mean that scholars have effectively renounced any effort to discover the real Jesus? I said earlier that they have renounced the search. I observe that most recent writing on the gospels does not attend to Jesus but to the separate presentations of Jesus by Matthew, Mark, Luke and John. What scholars are studying are several creative theological reconstructions. This means that to them what Jesus was is not important for the good reason that what he was cannot be known. What people thought he was is not only supremely important, it is the only thing of importance.

When we turn to Paul, the first Christian to put his beliefs in writing, we find with some surprise almost a lack of interest in the real historical Jesus. Paul had not experienced the real Jesus but he shows no sense of loss at the lack of this experience. He had experienced the risen living Jesus, of whom he said that God was in Christ reconciling the world to himself. Paul rarely quotes the words of Jesus, never directly, and never alludes to miracles or other deeds. Paul refers to nothing in the life of Jesus except his death and resurrection, if one may include the resurrection in the events of the life of Jesus. Paul proclaims nothing except the saving act of God in Christ. Had Christianity proceeded in the path set by Paul, it is hard to see how any of the gospels could have been written. In contrast to

The Real Jesus

Paul, the gospels appear as attempts to portray the real Jesus of history rather than the Christ of faith. Much of Christian art could never have been produced if nothing but Paul's gospel had been preached, yet modern scholars think that the gospels are four steps proceeding from Mark to John in the presentation of a Jesus never known or experienced by anyone.

This appears to be saying that the gospels reached through four steps the Christ of faith who was the only Christ ever known by Paul. But it is clear that the Christ of faith was not enough for many early Christians. By searching out and collecting memories where they were available and by the use of creative imagination where memory failed, the gospels produced a human figure with human traits—transfigured, it is true, but not yet the preexistent son of God and the risen glorified Lord. Yet it is these very gospels which modern scholars say stand between them and the real historical Jesus. Believers have been assured so often in recent years that the gospels are popular history that they are now not only uncertain of the meaning of the phrase but more than a little impatient of hearing it. Yet I beg the impatient to ask themselves how they, with their present equipment and capacity, would go about preparing a memorial notice of someone dead for thirty years or more whom they much admired, who received no attention from the press, who was recorded only in public records which they did not consult, and who lived only in the memories of his admirers and his enemies. Without training and experience in research and writing, what kind of notice would they produce? They would depend entirely on anecdotes. They would collect these anecdotes from the memories of the friends of their hero. They surely would not collect the memories of his enemies. They would arrange them as they thought best and it can be assumed that this would be an arrangement in which their hero would appear to best advantage. Their dates and their geography would be uncertain. In fact, their memorial notice would be much like a gospel.

Would this notice falsify the historical reality of their hero? It would be as faithful a presentation of the reality as they could make it. But one must admit that different people see different things in the same person. And the more complex and profound a person is, the greater the variety of views. Socrates was portrayed by three Greek writers, each of whom knew him personally. They give us three different persons. And there is a riddle of the real Socrates. The differences between Matthew, Mark and Luke are not as great. The Jesus of John is something of a different character. It seems wise not to approach the problem of the real Jesus as if a problem existed for no one else.

The Real Jesus

Lincoln's political opponents called him a baboon and it must be admitted that Lincoln was not endowed with physical beauty. If one searches for the real Jesus, one must find him in his words which the gospels at least appear to give us in abundance. But modern scholars approach even these with caution. It does not exaggerate this caution to say that they are not sure that we ever had the very words of Jesus.

More can be said than this, but before we say it let us notice some of the things which lead to the caution of scholars. Paul, the earliest Christian writer, quotes a saying of Jesus no more than once or twice and never, as we have mentioned, directly. It is safe to conclude that Paul did not have the words of Jesus to quote. Mark, the earliest of the gospels, has very few of the sayings of Jesus compared to Matthew and Luke. John, the latest of the gospels, has almost nothing except sayings of Jesus.

Scholars are sure, and I must plead that there is no time to explain it here, that almost none of the sayings of Jesus in the gospel of John come from Jesus himself. The conclusion suggests itself that early Christians did not remember much of what Jesus had said but that they often asked themselves what he would have said or must have said in this or that situation and that they expanded the sayings which were remembered. The process is not hard to understand. We who teach are often astonished, not to say alarmed, at what students sometimes quote as our sayings. Our own words are often expanded and interpreted rather than remembered. So much must be conceded to critical examination.

On the other hand, I have often been surprised by the stubborn refusal of many of my colleagues to admit that Jesus had at least as much skill, some would say magic, with words as Abraham Lincoln. One may wonder how Lincoln would have written if he had gone to Harvard. He would have written like other men who went to Harvard and we know how they wrote. He would have written like Emerson or Thoreau or Wendell Phillips. Or like Edward Everett, who wrote the quite forgettable two-hour speech which he delivered just before Lincoln's 288 words at Gettysburg. If Jesus had been trained as a rabbi, he would have sounded like a rabbi. And we can learn what they sounded like from the Talmud. The gospel of John quotes the temple police as saying that no one ever spoke as this man. Whether they said it or not, we can accept it. There is an original quality about the words of Jesus which cannot be traced back to biblical wisdom or scribal learning or rabbinical debate, and still less to Matthew, Mark and Luke. It is no dishonor to them to point out that they were second-rate minds. It is not for their high intelligence that they are read but for their preservation of sayings which they certainly never composed. There is, of course, an unmistakable flavor of village wit and wisdom about the sayings of Jesus. This does, in a way, help to authenticate them. If they sounded like the sayings of the Hellenistic philosophers, we could be reasonably certain that they did not come from Jesus. But even my colleagues have not suggested that the villages of Galilee were full of sages who tossed off lines like the Eight Beatitudes or the Parable of the Good Samaritan on demand.

Modern sophisticated city dwellers are often amused and fascinated by the homely folk wisdom of small towns and villages, the one-liners one can hear when one stops for gas or refreshments on a long trip. Journalists collect and publish them. One observes that they are one-liners and that when they are collected, they do not add up to a great deal. The sayings of Jesus are couched in this language. But they are much more than folk wisdom. One is, I am convinced, as close to the real Jesus as one can get when one reads the sayings of Jesus.

The words of Jesus in the gospels are teaching only in a very loose sense of the term. The sayings are scattered with no perceptible system nor even any arrangement imposed upon them by the authors of the gospels. In this un-structured arrangement, the sayings of Jesus resemble the sayings of the rabbis preserved in the Talmud, which is truly a random collection of sayings. The lack of arrangement also reflects the random quality of the memories preserved or the random quality of the expansions created by the disciples in answer to random questions. When one uses the word random collection of the sayings of Jesus, one has not said it all.

Christian doctrine is possible and has been produced from the very beginning of the church because the sayings exhibit certain recurrent themes. One may say, and some have said, that the recurring central themes are created by the collectors of the sayings and that they tell us little of the teaching of Jesus. This seems a bit strange. Certainly not all the sayings of Jesus were remembered, and probably very few of them were. The central themes exhibit that originality which we mentioned above as a quality of the form and style of the sayings. These themes are originally Christian. They are not derived from rabbinical teaching or traditional wisdom. Jesus often talked like a rabbi, or those who reported his words often made him sound like a rabbi. But it remains true that no rabbi ever talked like this man.

When one searches for the real Jesus, does one encounter Jesus the wonder worker, or is the wonder worker a pure product of legend? Several pertinent points can be made. One must candidly admit that there are several incredible features in the miracle stories and they do not always concern the miracle itself. One may instance the expulsion of the demons into the swine of Gerasa. Whatever is to be said of other details of the story, this detail is simply legendary. One must also admit candidly that miracles are much more frequently reported and believed in cultures more credulous than our own. I have never seen a miracle nor met anyone who had seen one. I should be glad to hear from anyone who has. Perhaps more significantly, I do not and never have included the possibility of a miracle in approaching any problem or making any plans. I do not think that my attitude is unusual. In the first century, however, there was a wonder worker of Asia Minor named Apollonius of Tyana of whom numerous miracles were reported. Resemblance between the miracles of Apollonius and the miracles of Jesus has often been noticed. No one believes the stories about Apollonius. Why are not the miracles of Jesus met with the same incredulity? Obviously, because Apollonius has never meant to anyone what Jesus has meant to so many. If Apollonius could be proved to have worked every miracle attributed to him, he would still be meaningless. This suggests that faith in Jesus is based on other things than miracles. It suggests that even if the historical value of each miracle account in the gospel were doubtful, there would still be ample motivation for faith in Jesus.

John L. McKenzie

Early Christians, some of them heretics, produced some imitation gospels called apocryphal gospels. Many of these show a fascination with the element of miracle which resulted in some exotic and repulsive stories of wonder-working power. Samantha, the witch of TV, is endowed with wonder-working powers. Desirous to join the community of normal human beings, she abstains from the use of this power except when she is under great pressure. The same gospels which relate the miracle stories present a Jesus who does not depend on this power in his daily life and who is not expected by the people who know him to employ this power as a usual procedure. There are exceptions but they are exceptions. Any kind of faith in Jesus tells us that he rose above the normal expected human behavior. This faith does not imply that Jesus was the village magician. In fact, any kind of faith in Jesus makes that impossible. The village magician could not be accepted as a member of the normal human community.

If Paul, the first Christian who wrote about Jesus, knew any of the miracle stories of the gospels, he does not refer to them. One may think that he did not regard them as important in his proclamation of Jesus. If he did not, he certainly differed sharply from almost all of those who have proclaimed Jesus since. Or one may think that Paul does not mention the micracles because he had never heard of them except the resurrection. Great men do collect stories of wonders. The stories are created by the admiration of their followers. They attest at least to the magnitude of the person of whom they were told: he was no ordinary man. The disciples believed that Jesus was no ordinary person. They do not attest that he walked in an atmosphere of wonder and terror of the unearthly power which was his at command. Those who were responsible for his death went about their task with no apprehension that this power would be invoked against them. His disciplies were profoundly scandalized that he could have let this happen.

If one believes that historical criticism permits one to say no more of the real Jesus than that he was an itinerant rabbi or a village sage dispensing folk wisdom about morality, one has not grasped the Jesus who evoked such stories. Not everyone has evoked them. The task is larger than the recovery of the real or historical Jesus.

There are really two problems. The first of these is the question whether the gospels present a credible figure and by this I mean a figure whom we recognize as a fellow member of the human community. The Christ of faith, especially in art and poetry, has often been a figure who really was not involved in the human condition, who could not be hurt by his human condition, who passed through the world without engagement in it. By a credible figure, I mean one who faces the problems of humanity with the resources of humanity. Unless he lives the human life and shares the human experience, he cannot tell me much about either.

The second problem is simply the problem that Jesus makes demands and promises which no one else makes. He asks a total commitment and promises a total fulfillment. He asks us to meet the demands with no resources which he did not have himself. He affirms that a God is involved in our human problems and that we cannot solve them without the resources which God makes available to us. To be credible, it is not enough that the real Jesus be an authentic human being. He must also be an authentic human being in whom, in the words of Paul, God was reconciling the world to himself. We do not know how much of the story of the conversion of Paul is memory and how much is legend. But the story does suggest that an encounter with the real Jesus is a revolution in one's personal life. This revolution happened to Paul without, as we have seen, any deep concern about the historical Jesus in the sense of concern about the details of the life of Jesus.

The Real Mary

WHEN I was asked to prepare a presentation on the real Mary, a presentation which would correspond to presentations on the real Jesus or the Jesus of history, my first inclination was to decline. The task is both too easy and too difficult.

It is too easy because, as I hope to explain, there is not enough information available to present the real Mary. It is too difficult because there is a Mary of popular belief. And while it is my duty as a professional scholar to point out, when I am asked, that the Mary of popular belief is a fictitious character, I can hardly expect to endear myself to many of my fellow Catholics by doing this duty.

Years ago I prepared an essay on the symbolic value of the legends of the Christmas season. It will be difficult to mount a similar effort for the legends of Mary. The solid information we have about the real Mary gives us her name, the name of her husband, and the fact of her motherhood of Jesus. For reasons which my colleague, Raymond Brown, has made clear at great length, it is impossible to use the infancy narratives of

Matthew and Luke as sources of authentic information about Mary. These narratives attest the early Christian belief that Jesus was the issue of virginal conception and that Mary is the mother of God. These beliefs give us no information about the real or the historical Mary, by which I mean that they tell us nothing about her as a person or about her life. Christian devotion from early times was dissatisfied with this meager recital. And Christian imagination began to create fiction about Mary.

Such fiction included the names of Mary's parents and the stories of her presentation in the temple and her betrothal and marriage to Joseph. These fictions are found in an early work which on all grounds is historically unreliable. And there is no reason why it should become reliable on such details as the names of Joachim and Anna (Hannah). Later in date are anecdotes which present Mary as the model of all Christian virtues. One does not question the virtue of Mary if one points out that one knows simply nothing of the way in which she fulfilled the obligations of virtue. I have mentioned the early belief in the divine maternity and the virginal conception attested in the infancy narratives of Matthew and Luke. One must point out that outside of these infancy narratives it is nowhere attested that Mary was aware of the divine maternity or of the virginal conception. Nor is any unusual understanding of the person and the mission of Jesus attested. The sources quote very few of the words of Mary directly and most of her words create an exegetical problem either in themselves or in the words of the person whom she addresses.

In Matthew, Mary is silent. In Luke, she speaks three times in the infancy narratives: once to an angel, once to Elizabeth and once to Jesus. Her words to an angel are not her words. Her words to Elizabeth are a recital of an early Jewish Christian hymn which we are sure Mary did not compose. Her words to Jesus express the typical complaint addressed by a mother to a wandering child. It is not without interest that Luke takes the trouble to state that Mary did not understand the explanation which Jesus gave of his wandering. In John, Mary speaks to Jesus once at the wedding feast of Cana. I reserve for further discussion a passage in which Mary, while not speaking, is associated with a group which does speak. No one will be surprised that we have the same problem about the very words of Mary that we have about the very words of Jesus. That is, we have no assurance that these are reports of what Mary said. This reservation has particular pertinence to the words of Mary as quoted in the infancy narratives and in the

Gospel of John where almost all of these quotations are found. In brief summary, we do not learn about the real Mary from her words.

The passage which I reserved for further discussion is found in Mark, Matthew and Luke. As usual, in such passages we take Mark's version as the original from which the others are derived. This practical rule has numerous exceptions which need not concern us here. Mark has the original version of this passage. The anecdote tells us that the Mother of Jesus and his kinsmen sought to see him while he was addressing a crowd. Jesus responded that his mother and his kinsmen were those who did the will of God. The request, probably it should be called a demand, to see Jesus follows a remark made by the same group a few verses earlier that Jesus is out of his mind and that they must go and seize him. Commentators generally believe that Matthew and Luke found this passage of Mark so harsh that they omitted it. Commentators have for centuries sought to exclude Mary from this statement about Jesus. In fact, the text does not expressly identify her with the opinion that Jesus is out of his mind. What she thought would not have been important. Decisions about such family crises were made by the adult males of the extended family. If this were the judgment passed upon Jesus by his kin, one should not be surprised that Jesus said that his family are those who do the will of God. Commentators have long sought to explain away the brusqueness of Jesus both in this passage and in the story of the wedding feast of Cana. Again, we should not lean too heavily on the text as containing the exact words of Jesus. Yet, those who wrote the text described him as speaking harshly in both instances, both by our standards of taste and by their own. In a considerable number of Gospel passages, Jesus imposes upon the disciples the duty of abandoning family relationships on the ground that these relationships are an obstacle to entering the realm of God. No one thinks that those texts arise from any personal experience of Jesus. Some scholars have suggested that they are not the words of Jesus but a response of early Christians to attempts made by those called the brethren of Jesus to claim some preeminence in the apostolic community. When one assembles the texts it becomes clear that Jesus never speaks in them of family relationships, either his own or in general, with warmth. Whether he ought so to have spoken of them, I do not know. Expressions of such warmth are rare in the Bible as they are in ancient literature generally. But they are not unknown.

One does not find the real Mary by painfully assembling from ancient sources the model of the village housewife. Those who are devoted to

Mary want to know the ways in which she was different from other women, not the ways in which she was typical. They would be closer to her if they knew better the ways in which she was unlike the sanitized, plastic housewives who appear in television commercials. Modern housewives would not be at home in Mary's one-room house with a dirt floor and no furniture except mats. Her day began at dawn with the grinding of the meal for the bread which she baked each morning. She carried water from the village well in a large jar placed on her head. It has often been noticed that this daily chore does wonderful things for the walk of village women. Her feet were normally bare. She did the family wash in the nearest pool or stream by literally beating out the dirt. She made most or all of the clothing that the family wore. The family's one meal was cooked over an open fire, made in the house when it rained. The normal village housewife could neither read nor write.

To find the real Mary, one must recognize that she lived a life of hard, routine drudgery within very narrow horizons. The millions of women who still live this way would, I fear, strike up a conversation with Mary in which common interests would be discovered much more quickly than the average housewife in the modern American city. And I hasten to point out that the modern housewife would not be improved by a

The Real Mary

sudden reduction in cultural status to the condition of an ancient village housewife. Modern civilization, too, produces conditions of life which are degrading. These conditions encourage people to become and to remain small. Such were the conditions in which Mary lived. They do not foster greatness.

In drawing a contrast between the real Mary and the modern "smart woman," as she is often called, I do not wish to imply that there was no such contrast in the world in which Mary lived. The New Testament mentions several contemporary smart laides: Herodias and her daughter, whose name, Salome, is mentioned by Josephus; Drusilla, Bernice and Pilate's unnamed wife. These ladies would have found no point of community with Mary. With the exception of Pilate's wife, of whom we know nothing, the rest of them were the kind of women whom the student of Latin letters encounters in the poets Horace, Ovid, Catullus, and Juvenal. Those who have not read these writers may rest assured that they are the same type of woman whom they encounter in gossip columns, television talk shows, and *People* magazine. Herodias, Bernice and Drusilla get more space in the New Testament than Mary does. They were wealthy, liberated and enlightened—and, shall I say, interesting?

I will venture the guess that some of the

women whom Paul mentions among his helpers or staff, who had little in common with the notorious courtesans mentioned above, would also have found little to talk about with an illiterate Palestinian housewife. I am suggesting that even in the church of Corinth where Paul said there were not many wise, noble or powerful, Mary would have been a cultural outsider. We have made her at home in our own church only by assimilating her to ourselves, and thereby destroying her.

For centuries, Christian art has found the Palestinian village housewife too unattractive for presentation. Even the titles by which she has been addressed remove her from her proper status. They all apply to her a word which is translated into English as "my lady," the respectful address given to a lady of quality. And a lady of quality Mary was not. Students of Greek point out that to address a woman simply as woman, as Jesus addresses Mary twice in the Gospel of John, is not a disrespectful address. Neither is it a sign of respect. It is neutral and could be given to a lady of quality or to a village housewife. This is not the implication of titles like madonna, madame, señora, and similar titles, the like of which were never given to the real Mary.

Christian artists have chosen for their models

The Real Mary

of Mary beautiful young women of Italy, France, Germany, Spain or other countries. Often they were the same young women who posed as Venus, Diana, or other goddesses. We know no more of the physical appearance of Mary than we do of the physical appearance of Jesus. We do know that women who bear their first child at fourteen and pass the rest of their lives at hard physical labor age prematurely. We do not know that Mary did so. We know that she lived the kind of life which normally has this effect.

One understands, one even sympathizes, with the Christian devotion which believes that the mother of Jesus, especially since she was free from sin, must have been the most beautiful of women. One also knows that the madonnas of Christian art are skillfully manufactured plastic dolls, with no relation to reality. It would have rewarded the artist to study closely the hands, wrists and forearms of women who grind meal every morning with a hand mill and who can hoist a water jar two feet tall to the top of their heads. The real Mary could have broken the arms of most of the artists.

It is not merely that the artists have failed to portray anything of what the real Mary may have looked like, it is rather that they have painted an imaginary Drusilla or Bernice—or, to mention another near contemporary of Mary,

Cleopatra. They could not have known that they were turning the Blessed Mother whom they venerated into a Barbie Doll.

Why did the artists and those for whom they painted do this to Mary? Several reasons come to mind. One is simple class snobbishness. The artist painted for the upper classes, and the upper classes were not ready to hang in the halls of their palaces a painting which looked like the scullery maid. If Mary was the greatest of women, she must be a member of that class which produced great women in the contemporary world. If she was a queen, she ought to look like a queen. And while queens in the Renaissance may have been less well endowed by nature than the chambermaid, they had far more art available to supply what nature had not given or to conceal nature's failure. Mary had to be painted as a woman who, when she entered a Renaissance ballroom, would immediately turn the eyes of the party from every other woman present. She had to be the kind of woman for whom the knight errant of chivalry would pledge his life and his honor. In that world, village housewives were not even people. And they were certainly not women who would even inspire the village laborer to pledge his life and his honor.

Another reason lies deeper and to bring it out is more chancy. Protestant controversialists up to quite recent times charge Roman Catholics with the idolatrous veneration of the Virgin, even with making her equal to God the Father and God the Son and God the Holy Spirit. It is, we know, dishonest to deny that superstition has always existed in the Roman Catholic church. Modern theologians are less sympathetic to what they regard as excesses of Mariological devotion in the past, even in the recent past. They find the dogma of the assumption of Mary somewhat difficult to explain. One hears no more of what was not long ago a vigorous campaign to promote the dogmatic declaration that Mary is the mediatrix of all grace. Some students of religion have suggested that the position of Mary in Roman Catholicism is due to the absence of the feminine element in Judaism and Christianity. The trouble with this theory is that it does not speak to the absence of the feminine element in Protestantism and Islam, neither of which has Mariology.

But the veneration of a goddess, the worship of the female principle, is so universal that its appearance needs no explanation. In the religions and culture of the ancient near East on which I could speak with some information, the worship of the female principle as a goddess was combined with the social degradation of women as a class. In ancient Israel the goddess was not worshiped but woman was a degraded social class. Certainly the exaggerated forms of the cult of Mary in Europe evoked echoes of the earth mother and the goddess of fertility. The older significance of the rites of May Day we do not communicate to children. If one pursues this line very far, one ends up more removed from the real Mary than when one studies Renaissance painters. Apart from what is clearly superstitious, one may suggest that the cult of Mary in historic European Christianity presented a feminine and, we may presume, a gentler side of the austere masculine religion of orthodox Christianity. But even in this severely restrained statement of the position, we are still removed from the real Mary. The real Mary in the New Testament is not a religious figure at all. In the infancy narratives she is at best a spokeswoman for early Christian belief.

We seem, then, to be dealing with a person who is totally unknown. What is told of her is a result of the play of fancy, either restrained, as in the infancy narratives of Matthew and Luke, or entirely unrestrained to the point of wildness, as in the ancient apocryphal gospels and in the legends of medieval and modern Mariology. History, it seems, gives us no more than the otherwise unknown mother of a famous man. Certainly the student of the famous man is tempted to search for the evidence of the influence of that person who was closest to him in the most pliable years of his life. For many other famous men besides Jesus the evidence is simply not available. If Lincoln did say that he owed all he was and had to his mother, the historian is unable to specify the indebtedness. There is ample evidence that mothers of famous men were often astonished by their sons. Christians have rarely felt restrained by evidence or its lack in attributing a great influence of Mary upon Jesus. This influence can neither be affirmed nor denied. It is safe to assume that Jesus learned from Mary those basic human skills which all boys learn from their mothers. Let others ennumerate what they think those skills are. I will mention the skill of learning to speak.

There are a few questions which in spite of the lack of information deserve a little more attention than I have given them. One of these is the personal mother-son relationship between Mary and Jesus. I have already noticed an apparent coolness in the record of these relations, scanty as the record is. Some scholars have concluded that the relations were as cool as the record. This is surely to go beyond the evidence. I am not fully read in the collection of Lincoln's writings but I believe that were it not for one chance remark which reveals warm filial devotion, one would conclude that relations between Lincoln and his mother were cool. But Lincoln made no remarks about the moral im-

John L. McKenzie

perative of detachment from family relationships. Jesus did. One might, if one wished to press the point, suggest that no one would mention the necessity of detachment from family relations who was himself totally unaware of family attachment. One may also argue that coldness between mother and son must stem from emotional or character defect in one or both. We have no right to assume this for either Jesus or Mary. And I must repeat that we have no assurance that we have anywhere a direct verbal report of the conversation. If we did, I am sure that I am not alone in knowing people whose casual behavior to each other conceals a very deep and devoted affection. Those who wish to think of Jesus and Mary as the very model of a loving and devoted mother and son are, as far as I know, free to think so. There is no reason to assume that their relation was anything but normal, whatever one thinks normal may be.

In Palestinian Judaism the fourth commandment was held in higher honor than it is in our own society. The son was obliged to obey his mother as long as he lived in her house. If he were the eldest or only son it was a sacred duty to support his mother as long as she lived. It is well known that this duty lies behind the commendation of Mary to the beloved disciple which is related in the fourth Gospel. Belief that Jesus and Mary enjoyed a model mother-son relationship is not well served, I think, by the invention of edifying incidents calculated to illustrate a personal relationship which we are sure existed but of which we have no evidence.

I have already indicated that a similar reserve must be exhibited towards the presentation of Mary as a model of Christian virtue. The only act of virtue which is recorded of Mary is her acceptance of the message of Gabriel. I have also indicated that my colleagues as a group do not believe that this is a record of an actual conversation. There are models of Christian virtue in the history and traditions of the church. And those who have lived as long as I have had opportunities to observe and live with authentic models of Christianity. As far as one can learn Christian virtue from what others have done, one can learn from these. From Mary I can learn nothing which is relevant to my problems in life. If I had to, I could mention others from whom I had at least a chance to learn. I know something about how they faced problems very similiar to those I have had to face. Of Mary and her problems and how she faced them and with what resources, I know nothing. If some popular beliefs about Mary were true, and I am sure they are not, there are some extremely common and pedestrian moral problems with which Mary was serenely unacquainted. I am

John L. McKenzie

sure she did know these problems but I do not know how she faced them.

The last question I choose for more extended discussion is Mary's understanding of the person and mission of Jesus. The only New Testament writer to mention this is Luke. And he says that Mary thought much about the events Luke related in his first two chapters. I have suggested that modern scholars have thought much about them too. They have concluded that they do not present much history to ponder. But even within his own framework, Luke is careful not to say that Mary understood what had happened. Christian belief has long cherished the assurance that Mary had an understanding of Jesus to which the solemn declarations of Nicaea, Ephesus, and Chalcedon could add nothing. It has been felt that Mary was the first and most perceptive of the disciples of Jesus and the one who believed most deeply. Of this assurance we must say, as we have said so often, that there is no evidence for it. The New Testament tells us nothing of how well Mary understood Jesus and his words. We may ask, as we did about mother-son relations, what assumptions we can make.

We can neither assume nor deny for Mary a high degree of intelligence. It is fairly safe to assume that religiously she was uneducated. This may not be important. Jesus himself is quoted more than once as saying that he and his words are hidden from the wise and the prudent and revealed to the simple. By these standards, Mary was capable of a full understanding of Jesus and his words. It would not have been an understanding which would have enabled her to grasp the declarations of Nicaea, Ephesus, and Chalcedon. I do not know that she had such an understanding. But I could have no quarrel with anyone who assumed that she had it. I do not know how Mary herself would have expressed verbally the understanding we assume that she had, for I share the assumption. As far as I know, words were not her game. I am again fairly sure that she could not have written a gospel and certainly nothing like the epistles of Paul. We may safely take Mary as a model of the faith of the simple. This includes the possibility that there were a great many things which she did not know.

In conclusion, in the course of the history of Christianity there have appeared heretics known as iconoclasts. These heretics believed that all uses of images in religious cult fell under the biblical prohibition of idolatry. And since they were fanatical in their beliefs, they roamed around the country smashing statues in churches. I suspect that the approach taken in this presentation will be called iconoclastic. It will be said that I am a smasher of innocent statues, a distorter of art which has given so many generations of Christians religious joy and comfort and left them nothing but the mere crusts of historical evidence on which to feed their piety. Is it the destiny of Mont St. Michel and Chartres to perish under the critic's hammer? The question is legitimate. At the risk of flippancy, I recall a popular song of some years ago in which the unhappy lover sought a paper doll which he could call his own in preference to a real live girl. Beautiful, the madonna may be, queenly, holy, wise, and, to sum up in the words of a late professor of theology, you may call her anything except God. But she is a paper doll. She is a caricature, however artistic, of something which never existed. She has suffered at the hands of those who venerate her the same thing which happened to Jesus. The real Jesus and the real Mary are not nice enough, not pretty enough, for veneration in their reality. They come from the wrong side of town and they are not, you know, our kind of people. But if we fluff them up with enough gilt and plaster, they will look enough like us to be acceptable.

Possibly I exaggerate when I say that we reject the real Mary and replace her with a plastic doll because we could not invite her into our homes as our social equal. Very few people know the real Mary well enough to reject her.

The Real Mary

And the rejection is not conscious and deliberate. Can anyone be blamed for framing an imaginary Mary who is like the people we are? Is it not a function of art to idealize the image of those who are loved and venerated? Indeed it is. And if it were not more than a matter of transfiguring the real Mary with a physical beauty I am sure she did not have (at least I am sure it was not Italian or French), I should be more tolerant of a human failure. But the rejection of a social and economic class to which Mary belonged is both conscious and deliberate, no less so because it is habitual and shared by so many. This rejection is one of the features of human society against which some of the strongest words attributed to Jesus in the gospels are directed. So considered, much of traditional devotion to Mary has to be judged idolatrous.

I admit that the real Mary would not elicit the art and music which the plastic Mary has elicited. But if we cannot take her in her reality, we might honor her better if we left her in the obscurity in which the New Testament left her.

Myths in the Bible

THE question of myth in the Bible up to quite recent times was solved by many scholars who denied that there is any myth in the Bible. The reasons for this denial lie in the fear that myth is a falsehood and they did not feel they could safely admit falsehoods, however innocent, in the Bible.

In the present generation, we are much more ready to accept the use of myth in the Bible because we do not believe that the myth necessarily is falsehood. Nor do we feel that the Bible must be in every line entirely faithful to historical memory. It is not in many instances, and myth is only one of these instances. What we know about myth is that it does not pretend to be a history. It is an attempt to explain something which lies to some extent outside of human experience. The world, for instance, in which we live does not lie outside of human experience but its origins do lie outside that experience. There is no memory of the origin of the world. Most races of men have dealt with this question and most of them have dealt with it through a myth which explains the origin of the world.

The myth is always a story. On examination, the story presented as a single event turns out to be a poetic description of some enduring feature in nature or in human institutions. Thus, for instance, the cycle of the seasons recurs annually. It is not, in the historical sense of the word, an event. It is constant and during most of modern history man takes the succession of the seasons for granted. It is not unexpected. It is not something which he feels threatens him. Ancient man apparently was not so sure that the seasons would regularly return in the proper order. To them it seemed each year was an event. Nature had remained faithful to its known patterns and they attributed this to the work of some will more powerful than the will of man which governed the succession of the seasons. But since, at least in the temperate zone, the succession of the seasons seems to be the result of conflicting forces such as the moist and the dry, the hot and the cold, it was necessary to tell a story in which these conflicting forces appeared as conflicting persons. And so the myth of the seasons issued in the story of a conflict of divine beings of which one or one group expressed the orderly processes of nature and the other what appears to man to be disorderly processes which threaten the security of man and the regularity of nature. Such, for instance, is a storm which can be both a benevolent force and a destructive force. Such a paradox man recognizes in himself and so he attributes these natural forces to a kind of being who exhibits the unpredictability which man sees in himself.

Myth, in this and other areas, is an attempt to explain reality. The explanation is not that which in modern times is sought by philosophical or scientific method. Ancient man was not acquainted with these processes of thought and his explanation to us seems to be childish. What he sought was a way of describing nature which made it possible for him to live with it. The myth of the succession of the seasons or of the process of fertility is a myth of life and death. Death to man has generally been the supreme irrational factor of human life. It is difficult to explain why a man begins to live. Once he does begin, it becomes impossible to explain why he ceases to live. Ancient man did not pretend to explain death but merely to make it possible to accept his mortality without daily falling into a pit of depression over it. So the myth of the succession of the seasons is the myth of the eternal recurrence of life, not indeed in the individual but in the universe in which man lives. Life endures even if the individual person does not. And this, to some extent, made it possible for man to live with his own mortality, and even to accept life as a gift graciously given by a benevolent God and intended to be enjoyed for a limited period of time. Man reconciled himself with his mortality by acknowledging that he was not a god and that immortality was proper to the gods. Implicitly they also meant that it was proper to the nature in which man lives.

An explanation of any event or phenomenon by means of a story may be a true explanation and may be a false explanation. In modern times, we believers think that a story of nature which explains nature as the conflict of different gods is a false explanation because our own belief and our own theology do not permit us to accept the hypothesis of a number of gods. We seek another explanation. So did the ancient Israelites who also did not believe in many gods.

What the ancient Israelites sought was not a theology but another myth which would explain the universe as an event, a story, which was the work of only one supreme being. Such is the Israelite myth of creation. This idea of myth can be well shown in the story of the fall of man, the story of Eden and of Adam and Eve. Space does not permit a complete discussion of the reasons why scholars are convinced that this narrative cannot be historical. Many readers have had the suspicion without going through all the details through which the scholar would take them. The account has certain incredible features, such as a talking serpent. There is in modern times the question of a memory of any event which could be preserved through the hundreds of thousands of years (at least) which we now reckon as having elapsed since man first appeared on the earth. But we can be quite certain that the author of the account of Eden did not intend to write a history in the same sense in which another biblical author intended to write the story of David and Bathsheba. The two events were not the same in the minds of their writers nor of their readers.

Again, there are certain features in the narrative which we believe would manifest to the readers or the hearers the purpose of the author and his intention to communicate something else than a simple historical memory of events. Such features can be found in almost all literatures. In English, a story which begins with the phrase, "once upon a time in a country far away," is recognized by the readers to be a fictitious account which is placed in no date and in no place. It is the work of imagination. A myth, likewise, is manifestly a work of imagination. It is the use of symbolism to explain a reality which creates the problem. In most mythology the modern reader is outside the symbolism which was common at the time the myth was composed. He may fail to understand or misunderstand the symbol which is employed.

John L. McKenzie

Certain discoveries about the ancient world now make these symbols more clear to us, although we should not pretend that we can share the understanding of the storyteller and his readers at the time the narrative was composed.

The problem which the myth of Eden faces can be called the problem of the human condition, more specifically, the failure of man to integrate himself totally with his surroundings in nature and with his fellowmen. One should recall at this point that the story of Eden is the first of a whole series of stories running from Genesis, chapter II through chapter XI, which deals with the human condition. Chapters II and III state, in the form of a story, that the human condition as man knows it was not the work of the creative deity, that man did not suffer originally from some difficulties, pains and dangers which are now routine in his life. That a life is described free of these dangers in some terms rather than others depends on the culture in which the writer's imagination works.

Modern man would not describe an ideal troublefree state as life in a garden where the ground produced enough food with very little labor and no fear of failure. He probably would not describe the ideal human relations as Genesis does, in almost the terms of two children rather than two adults. Yet it has long been known both in history and mythology that growth to human adulthood is often a growth in malice. To this extent the ancient interpreters were at least partly right in thinking that the story of Eden presented the original human couple as children, at least in innocence, and that complete adulthood came only with the malice of their deed.

What the author regarded as the basic fall of man, a fault which changed the human condition from an ideal state, whatever it was, into the historical state, has never been clearly defined. Certainly the author meant some kind of rebellion against the will of God. This rebellion is expressed in the symbolism of the story which is very largely sexual. I'm not referring merely to the nudity of the couple and their discovery that decency demands that they wear clothing. I am referring more to the symbolism of the serpent which we can now define with some clarity in the ancient world of art and literature. The symbolism of the serpent is not uniform throughout the ancient near east. One can say clearly that is often associated with the female figure who is the goddess of fertility. The narrative of Genesis suggests this symbolism which we see in art and it seems gratuitous to say that neither the author nor his Israelite listeners were unaware of this symbolism rather widespread in the artistic remains of the ancient near east.

We feel even more security when we recognize that the symbolism of the nude goddess and the serpent was a part of that cult of fertility which the Bible so often mentions as a prevailing superstition into which the Israelites fell so frequently. And one cannot be far from the truth, even if one has not obtained a complete understanding, if one believes that the story of Genesis is to some extent a polemic against this cult of fertility and that it attributes the human condition with its pains and its issue in death to this superstitious cult.

Putting it in the larger context of these chapters, one feels even more certainty that the writer presents this superstitious cult as the radical evil from which all later evils, such as the murder of brother by brother, the annihilation of man by the wrath of God in the deluge, and the building of the first city as an expression of human pride and vanity follow. One must, it seems, seek for some such explanation as this once it becomes clear that the writer cannot have been dealing with historical memory. The story as a myth does make sense. It is an Israelite effort to explain the condition of man in terms of Israelite belief, to place the fault of man precisely where it belongs, at the door of man himself and not the door of some malicious deity. That it makes the human condition totally intelligible hardly any reader would say. But the believer has always accepted this myth as at least a step towards making the human condition tolerable and, as we observed earlier, this is more or less all that the myth proposed to do.

In Christian belief the story of Eden has received new interpretations which were almost certainly not in the mind of the original writer nor of the original readers and hearers. It is not possible, again, to discuss all of these in the space alloted us. But it should be mentioned that the myth of Eden is not a proposition of a belief in original sin as this belief is defined in Catholic teaching. This is a development of belief which is based on the story of Eden but which goes notably beyond the story.

That man suffers from a kind of inherent perversion which makes it almost certain that he will do wrong rather than right is a view of the human condition which paraphrases the story of Eden. Such a paraphrase would not be satisfactory as a definition of the Christian view of original sin, which is much more precise and which is based more on the writings of Paul in the epistle to the Romans than it is on the text of Genesis. We said that the story is a myth. Paul in his treatment of original sin departs from the myth but arrives at a theological statement of his belief, a statement which we simply do not find in the story. It is a part of the function of myth in societies which depend on myth for the understanding of God in nature that the myth raises questions as well as answers them. It leads the listener to ask himself new questions about his place in the world, his place before the deity, which he would not have asked had he not heard the myth.

Let us turn now to another example of the imaginative treatment of events which is not properly mythological and very probably should not be included in the same discussion with Genesis. Yet I believe I am not entirely false either to the Bible or to understanding of myth if I take these two together since they have at least in common that they are imaginative creations with the purpose of giving their readers and their hearers a deeper understanding of a religious event and of their own belief in the deity. I have reference to the problem of the gospel accounts of the birth of Jesus.

Certain substantial differences between this problem and the problem of the origin of man should be stated at once and clearly. In the birth of Jesus we are not dealing with events which lie beyond the capacity of human memory. The birth of Jesus occurred in historical times in a time and place which are the objects not only of historical memory but even of written records. Even if we cannot give an exact date of the birth of Jesus it must have fallen within the space of a few years in a period of history which is fairly well known. The reality of the birth of Jesus is not a mythological event. The birth of Jesus is a historical event even though it cannot be dated precisely. The historical reality of the birth of Jesus does not depend on the historical quality of the narratives in which this birth is related.

Historical events quite often are presented in a manner which is not faithful to history. A celebrated painting of Washington crossing the Delaware represents an historical event in a visible form in which it could not possibly have occurred. Yet no one doubts that he crossed the Delaware on the occasion which the picture intends to represent. One may compare this highly imaginative and historically unfaithful presentation of an event in the life of George Washington to artistic presentations of the nativity of Jesus. Hardly any event of the gospels has been so popular with Christian artists as the nativity. I have seen, I suppose, hundreds of such representations, as most of us have. Many have been produced by some of the most celebrated artists of the Renaissance and modern times. I have never seen one that bore what I as a historian could regard as even a remote resemblance to the event as it must have occurred.

Since so many celebrated painters are Italian,

the landscape is usually Italian rather than Palestinian. The buildings which they present in the background are Italian renaissance buildings rather than Palestinian structures of Hellenistic times. The costumes of all except the major figures in the paintings are costumes of the 15th or 16th century. The major figures, Jesus, Mary and Joseph, if we may include the infant as a major figure, wear costumes which were really never worn by anyone. They were the artist's idea of what people of the period wore. One may speak of this as infidelity to history. One must also notice that it is rather faithful to a belief. Christians believe that the nativity, like the whole life of Jesus, is an enduring event contemporary to all times. The birth of Jesus is equally significant to all men no matter when or where they lived. The result of the symbolism of the artists is to place the nativity in their own time and in their own country as contemporary event. This is a theological dimension of the nativity, not a historical dimension, and in order to express the theological dimension, the artist had to renounce the historical dimension. Little was lost, since they could not have painted a historical representation in any case.

We do not regard such paintings as a distortion of history, much less of theology. We allow the artist certain liberties to represent an event which neither he nor we have witnessed. We allow him the use of symbolism. We admit that the arts of painting and sculpture can convey meaning which photography is not able to convey. The meaning ultimately is the insight of the artist himself into the event which he paints and he can only express this insight through symbolism, not by being entirely faithful to the visual reality of the event with which he is concerned.

There is a symbolism of literature as well as a symbolism of painting and sculpture. We accept poetry as a form of literature which is a vehicle of truth. The truth which poetry conveys is not the truth of historical narrative. We do not expect it to be and we do not find fault with poetry that it does not represent history. What is the truth of Hamlet? One cannot answer this question in merely historical terms and say anything meaningful about Hamlet.

The fact that we accept poetry as a legitimate form of expression does not, however, mean that we are ready to accept poetry in the Bible and particularly in such things as the infancy narratives. And one who hears the suggestion is entitled to ask why the interpreter believes that the narratives are poetry rather than history. The interpreter has this belief because of questions which arise from the narrative itself. On the hypothesis that the narrative of the infancy is of the same historical quality as the narrative of the crucifixion, which itself raises problems, certain historical problems arise which the interpreter in our present state of knowledge finds impossible to solve. A brief statement of these problems with no attempt to answer them will make it clear why the interpreter looks into the possibility of a symbolic and artistic interpretation rather than historical interpretation.

One wonders why Matthew and Luke are completely independent of each other and why, in the last analysis, they cannot be harmonized. Matthew knows nothing of a previous residence in Nazareth of the parents of Jesus. Luke does know about it. Luke knows nothing of the killing of the innocents and the flight into Egypt and it cannot be inserted into the gospel of Luke without seriously distorting the presentation. Luke brings Joseph and Mary to Bethlehem because of a census. Matthew knows nothing of this census. As far as our historical knowledge at the present goes, Matthew is quite correct. There was no census at any possible date which he could have known of and one must, as far as the census goes, suppose that Luke, or more probably his sources, remembered the census but did not remember the time at which it occurred. For Luke it was an easy way to reconcile the birth of Jesus in Bethlehem with the known residence of Jesus in Nazareth. Unfortunately, Luke may have placed the couple in Bethlehem for the census in virtue of a nonexistent law. We have no indication that in the Roman census at this time anyone was required to go to the town of his ancestors in order to register.

These are merely questions, not answers. But they are questions which must be dealt with by anyone who asserts that Matthew and Luke together give an historical account of the birth of Jesus. They do permit another who finds it impossible to deal with the gospels in these terms to suggest that nothing was known of the birth of Jesus at the time the gospels were written. This is not incredible. As noted earlier, little is known as a rule of the birth of anyone. It is a matter of interest only to his immediate family; and if the person becomes in adult life a person of historical importance, the facts of his birth and infancy, if they are known at all, are known only because he was a member of a celebrated family which was accustomed to expect that its members would be persons of historical importance, at least minor figures.

When the time came to write the gospels, the author of first gospel, Mark, felt no obligation to

John L. McKenzie

treat the birth and infancy of Jesus. It does not occur in Mark for what seems to be the very good reason that Mark had no information. If Mark did not have information on these topics, we have to ask ourselves where Matthew and Luke may have received it. I am aware of a devout legend that Luke sat at the knees of Mary, notebook in hand, and wrote down her own memories of this great event in her life. This is indeed a devout, even a beautiful, scene but it cannot be verified historically. One is forced to ask at this point what language they would have spoken which they both had in common; and if one accepts the hypothesis that Luke sat at the feet of Mary to get his story, one has to ask at whose feet Matthew sat to get his, which is quite different. It does not, therefore, seem to be an entirely unreasonable suggestion that these two evangelists, lacking historical information about the birth of Jesus, created the event by the use of imagination.

If we ask why they did this, the narrative itself reveals their purpose. Both evangelists mean to affirm that Jesus is the Messiah and his messiahship, indeed his royal messiahship, was manifest in his nativity. This is not affirming an historical falsehood. It is affirming a belief which was secure in the apostolic church through an imaginative presentation of an event of which there was no historical presentation. History, including here the gospels themselves, do not permit us to accept the infancy and early life of Jesus as lived in an atmosphere of wonder. The nativity wonders have no echo anywhere in the gospels. This of itself would not allow us to deny their historical character but it does allow us to raise questions.

That Jesus was the Messiah was a basic article of early Christian faith. There are many ways in which this can be stated. The New Testament uses many ways of stating it. No one except Matthew and Luke employ imaginative narrative to state it. But it is affirmed and in both Matthew and Luke the unbelief of those near the Messiah is contrasted with the belief of those who are more remote from him. In Matthew, it is the travelers from the east. In Luke, it is the poor as opposed to the wealthy and religious leaders. This is the theme which recurs in the gospels. This has an echo. And we believe that Matthew and Luke intended to present this miracle of faith in the very beginning of the life of Jesus.

It is again not without interest that such explicit claims that Jesus is the Messiah are not found in the words of Jesus himself as the gospels have reported them. Jesus' attitude towards his Messiahship has to be described as extremely reserved. It is reserved even with those who are closest to him. And such an explicit display as we have in both Matthew and Luke is not entirely in harmony with the proclamation of Jesus himself. It is in harmony with the very explicit faith of the early Christian community and it appears that this is the best place in which to put it.

The religious symbolism of the nativity story reflected now in the liturgical cycle of the nativity feast is full of meaning and makes it quite possible for the scholar who has his doubts about the historical character of the nativity accounts to participate fully in the nativity liturgy, since he shares the faith of Matthew and Luke and his fellow-believers in Jesus Messiah. This faith is first granted in these stories to the poor and the lowly and, from the point of view of Jewish learning, the ignorant. If he is to share this faith, these are the people with whom he must join himself. He feels it may possibly be good for him to do so and that even the artistic and literary symbolism of a nativity scene can be shared only by those who are willing to share it with the shepherds and the strangers.

Another question concerns the three strange visitors from an unknown country who, in the story of Matthew, have learned of the birth of the king Messiah by watching the heavens. The country from which these men came, while not mentioned by Matthew, can be mentioned by the modern scholar. It has to be Mesopotamia. The people known in the Old Testament as the Chaldeans who lived in southern Mesopotamia had by New Testament times given their name to a trade. Chaldeans were astrologers. And what Matthew describes is the visit of three astrologers who have learned of the event from studying the heavens. I will not say that one has to believe in astrology to believe in the historical character of the wise men; but this is certainly what the wise men are presented as being. The event occurs during the reign of the celebrated Herod the Great. In the chronology in use since the 6th century, Herod the Great died four years before the birth of Jesus. This is not an insoluble difficulty, surprising as this may be, since the chronology now in use which makes this the year 1981 is by no means certain and the birth of Jesus might well have occurred before the death of Herod. The problem is complicated by the fact that no historical source except Matthew has the story of the killing of the innocents. Our only information about Herod besides the New Testament comes from the Jewish historian Josephus. That Josephus does not mention this does not of course prove it did not happen. Josephus may have had his own reasons for omitting it, among them possibly the fact that the event was unknown to him. What does arouse some wonder is the fact that Josephus manifests a deep and sincere hatred for Herod the Great and all his works. As far as we can see, he not only omits no crime which was credited to Herod, he possibly includes a few for which Herod was not responsible. There is no good reason why Josephus should have omitted this story except that he did not know it. And again, we must face the question whether Josephus did not know about this event because it never happened.

The Book of Revelation

THE Book of Revelation, which Catholics have long been accustomed to call the Apocalypse, is not the most read book of the Bible although it is one of the books which is most discussed, at least over a long period of history. Anyone who has looked into the book even casually probably experienced a feeling of paralysis in the mind. From beginning to end the book seems to convey nothing but obscurity. The writer uses words and images, but the reader of the Bible feels that the meaning of the author escapes him. This use of images belongs to a type of literature which was quite common at the time the Book of Revelation was written. The type appears in Jewish literature even before Christian times and there are other examples of this type of writing which did not find their way into the New Testament.

This type of writing is called apocalyptic and in general it presents the end of the world as a great catastrophe involving the whole world and the entire human race. It is an act in which God pronounces judgment upon the wicked and vindicates the righteous. The images in which this judgment and vindication occur run to certain types which can be seen in most of the apocalyptic books. In this area, the Book of Revelation does not differ notably from earlier writings. The reader will have noticed the use of numbers—for instance, the numbers 7, 10 and 12. These have a generally uniform meaning. The number 7 indicates perfection or completeness. Thus the letter to the seven churches of Asia Minor is really a letter to the whole church. The number 12 represents generally Israel or the church of the new Israel and is derived from the twelve tribes of Israel. The number 10 also signifies a type of fullness and especially multiples of 10 indicate not only fullness but immensity, as the number 1,000 which occurs several times in the Book of Revelation. The number 4 indicates the world, either the four points of the compass or the four elements.

The images of judgment are lurid. Death and destruction occur in forms which for the ancient mind were exaggerated beyond all reality. It is not surprising that some modern readers, when they compare the Book of Revelation with the instruments of destruction devised in modern warfare sometimes wonder whether the fulfillment of the Book of Revelation is not at hand. Without attempting to take anything away from the catastrophic destruction which modern war inflicts, it is quite safe to say that this is not what the writer of the Book of Revelation had in mind.

The vindication of the righteous takes a somewhat ambiguous form. This occurs in the final chapters of the book in the form of the New Jerusalem. But the New Jerusalem is really two Jerusalems. One is a heavenly city; the other is an earthly city. In each of them, the New Jerusalem is the city where God finally and permanently dwells with the righteous. The purpose of this type of literature can be understood against its historical background. Both in Judaism and in Christianity apocalyptic literature was created in religious groups which felt themselves to be historically helpless. The Israel and Judah which lived under the monarchies from the 9th to the 6th centuries were independent and sovereign states having the capacity of self-determination which we attribute to such sovereign states. After the 6th century, Judaism became a religion and ceased to be a political reality. It was politically inactive in the face of the great powers of the ancient world. This inactivity was continued in the early Christian church which was so unimportant in the Roman empire that we scarcely find it mentioned by Latin writers for the first two hundred years of its existence.

This feeling of helplessness convinced the

group that it could not hope to achieve anything by means of political power or influence. It could look only to the acts of God and these acts are described in the apocalyptic literature. But it was not sufficient merely to point to events in history or in nature and identify these as the saving and judging acts of God. It was necessary that the acts of God be manifestly his acts and not mere accidents of history. God owed it to himself to reveal his justice to the nations and to reveal it in such a manner that it exceeded in its dimensions any merely human act of judgment. If the power of God is to be revealed it must be revealed on a scale which makes it impossible to think of it as the power of anyone else. Hence, the exaggerated display of judgment which we see in the Book of Revelation was for its writer and its readers a necessary consequence of their belief in the supremacy of God.

If God is truly supreme, he must show this supremacy and he must show it in a way which will silence every objector. Since history manifested no reality corresponding to judgment as the apocalyptic writers conceived it, they had to appeal to images which were derived from nature and from history but which went far beyond any known experience of man. Thus, the angels with the seven trumpets: by the sound of the trumpets, hail and fire which destroy a third of the earth, a flaming mountain which falls into the sea and destroys a third of the life in the sea, a great star which falls from heaven and destroys a third of the waters of the streams, a darkening of a third of the sun and the moon and the stars, a falling star which turns out to be a demonic being who opens the shaft of the bottomless pit from which a great cloud of black smoke emerges, locusts which emerge from the smoke and destory living beings and which have a monstrous appearance, and apocalyptic battle between the forces of evil and the forces of good, and a notice that the trumpet of the seventh angel will introduce genuine catastrophe to which the preceding is merely an introduction.

These dreadful events are somewhat duplicated elsewhere in the book but it is clear that what the writer wishes to describe is a world catastrophe. Of this catastrophe, he had no experience. He could describe it only by the use of his imagination, basing his imagination largely upon biblical writings and apocalyptic writings of Judaism. The description of the salvation and the vindication of the righteous is less vigorous than the symbolism of judgment, no doubt because the imagination proceeds much more easily in describing catastrophe than it does in describing eternal bliss. This has always been difficult for believers to interpret. But if the reader reflects on the catastrophe which the writer describes, he may wonder whether the attitude which the writer shows towards the wicked and an unmistakable glee which he shows in describing their dreadful end is not perhaps more vindictive than one would expect in a Christian. This, it seems, must be admitted. And it also demands some explanation.

We have remarked on the feeling of helplessness which Christians felt in the face of the world. In the concrete, the world which they faced was the Roman Empire and it is difficult for us in modern times to reconstruct the sense of political power which the empire manifested towards its members. At the time of the writing of the Book of Revelation there was really no other political power worth counting in the world. The Roman Empire was supreme as no state has been supreme either before or since. The Christians had no difficulty in identifying the empire with an antiGod and an antiChrist. However the idea of the antiChrist is to be explained in detail, it must in some sense refer to the Roman Empire. This feeling about the empire did not arise until the empire persecuted the Christians. And this occurred for the first time in the reign of Nero in Rome.

It does not seem that Nero's persecution extended beyond Rome. But in the reign of Domitian in the last decade of the first century, persecution was more widespread and for this reason critics usually date the composition of the Book of Revelation in this period. They see no event to which the book is a proper response except the persecution of Domitian. Furthermore, Domitian insisted on asserting his own divinity, the divinity of the emperor, in a way which went beyond the somewhat conventional emperor worship which had been practiced during most of the first century.

Christians found this extremely offensive. Such a being was readily conceived, as we have noticed, as a genuine antiGod who was endowed with all the power of the world. No power could be matched with the power of the emperor-God except the power of the heavenly God. And if it were to prove itself supreme power, it had to manifest itself as able to overcome the power of Rome. This is the event which the writer described in images.

Since no human power could be invoked to overthrow Rome, the writer employs the armies of nature and the heavenly host as the enemies whom Rome ultimately cannot vanquish. Nor does the writer, like the other New Testament writers, see any Christian empire which will replace the empire of Rome. When Rome falls, the Kingdom of God will be revealed and God will dwell in his kingdom in the New Jerusalem.

Certainly the writer had no idea of the subsequent extent of the history of Christianity. Apocalyptic writers, and indeed all New

Testament writers, who touch upon the subject of the end of time generally disclosed their own belief that this end cannot be very far removed. To recognize Rome as an antiGod hostile to the Christian community may explain the vindictiveness which the writer shows, but it does not justify it. This type of hostility to the wicked is not the attitude which Jesus himself exhibits and teaches in the gospels. And the position of Christians before the world cannot be simply the position of the writer of the Book of Revelation and still call itself Christian. Christians should have no problem understanding the vindictiveness of the writer since they have proved themselves capable of showing the same sentiment. But it cannot be justified by an appeal to the Book of Revelation without making the gospels somewhat irrelevant to one's Christian attitude towards one's enemies.

It is true that the writer of the Book of Revelation does not think of doing anything himself or of his fellow Christians being active in bringing down the enemy of God. God himself will do this. It is his privilege to dream how God will bring it about. But his ideas can only be called dreams. The judgment of God takes forms which are more frequently unpredictable than predictable. The writer has a conviction that if God is to demonstrate his supremacy he must finally overcome evil and vindicate good. No one can quarrel with this belief if he believes in God at all. But when we begin to write directions on how God is to manifest his supremacy, we may produce a human idea of divine supremacy rather than the truth. In this sense it must be admitted that the apocalyptic literature, including the Book of Revelation, can be, and has been, misleading.

It is always necessary to take the entire New Testament into account when one speaks of Christian belief. It is particularly necessary when one deals with the Book of Revelation. How is one to think of the judgment of God in the end of history? If we are compelled by sound interpretation to judge that the Book of Revelation is an image of judgment rather than its reality, how are we to represent to ourselves the reality of judgment? Is it possible that we may doubt that God will ultimately and finally manifest himself? At many times in history Christians have been ready to believe that the end is at hand. These sentiments have arisen usually in times of crisis when the very fabric of civilization seems to be threatened.

An exception may be made for the period of about 1000 of our era. The use of the period of 1000 years in the Book of Revelation led many, although not the majority, of Christians in the 10th century to believe that the world would end with the year 1000. This was an aberration, it was not widespread, and when the year 1000 passed without any visible end of the world, the idea, it would seem, should have disappeared. In fact, while I personally do not expect to be present for it, I rather expect that the approach of the year 2000 will create among believers a rather similar uncertainty and, in some circles, panic. Such diversions arise from taking the Book of Revelation too literally and one may complain because when the Book is interpreted too literally, other authentic features of Christianity are obscured by a concentration on judgment and salvation, particularly on the destruction of the wicked, our enemies, and the reward of the righteous, ourselves.

Apocalyptic literature, including the Book of Revelation, leads to the view of Christianity as an elite which has very little to do with history and the progress of events, which is inactive and which need not be active. Christians can afford to hide and await their vindication in the great act of God. It does tend to relieve the Christian of a sense of his responsibility towards the world and his fellowman, the kind of responsibility of which Jesus spoke when he urged that the ultimate test of belief in his disciples would be the feeding of the hungry, the clothing of the naked, the harboring of the shelterless and the visiting of the sick and those in prison. The one whose mind is deeply fixed on the end of time can afford to neglect these activities as being merely temporary substitutes for the ultimate reality.

Our question of how we ourselves are to think of the end of time remains unanswered. Perhaps, at least in this generation, indeed in this phase of our civilization, it is not possible to answer it as definitely as the writer of the Book of Revelation attempted to answer it. Our faith in the final vindication of God must be as firm as the faith of the writer of the Book of Revelation. Most of us find his images unsympathetic. Even though a world catastrophe can be imagined, it is not necessary to imagine it in the terms employed by the Book of Revelation. With the growth of our own knowledge of the world and of men, the image of the world catastrophe is more difficult to sustain than it was for the writer of the book who lived in a smaller world.

The imagery in which our own apocalyptic vision will be formed has not yet been created. This does not mean that no imagery is valid. A conviction that there must be a permanent and irreconcilable opposition between good and evil follows from any belief in God. Our own difficulty in distinguishing the two both in theory and in practice is not representative of the permanent state of mankind, we hope, nor even of man at his potential best as we ourselves can see him. Such a belief does not necessarily issue in the kind of judgment which the Book of Revelation presents. The kind of judgment which will demonstrate this beyond all doubt at the moment is hidden from us.

The ultimate value, it seems, of the Book of Revelation is this basic conviction that God must justify himself. There are many ways in which this conviction can be expressed. Revelation is one. We perhaps have not found ways for ourselves which are equally convincing either to ourselves or to unbelievers. There is a common feeling in the world that God, if he exists, is rather helpless in the face of events, in fact, that God himself must also wait for an apocalypse. But of course, it is impossible to think of him awaiting it. The writer of the Book of Revelation had no such doubt. On the other hand, it is not clear that he convinced very many people that his image really represented the reality. So perhaps, while we await the invention of our own apocalyptic imagery, it may be wiser to return to the imagery of the gospels and to see the coming of the Son of Man in the presence in the world of those who do feed the hungry, give drink to the thirsty, clothe the naked and harbor the harborless. Ultimately it appears this attitude will convince people of the ultimate and irreconcilable difference between good and evil in a way in which no other teaching can convince them.

The Book of Job

ONCE upon a time, in the land of Uz, there was a man named Job who exhibited the unusual combination of great wealth and great virtue. He was a rancher, we would call him, the owner of thousands of animals. He was the faithful husband of one wife and the father of ten children and he was a sincerely religious man who fulfilled scrup lously his obligations of worship. And he was all of this in spite of the fact that by any standards he and his family were members of the leisured class.

So remarkable was he that God once boasted about him to the adversary, for that is what Satan means, who seems to have been a kind of heavenly grand inquisitor or inspector general whose business it was to doubt the sincerity of alleged virtue. The adversary responded that Job's virtue was no wonder for he had never known anything but God's favor. If he were tested by adversity he might not hold up.

Very well, said God, test him with adversity, anything short of death. And tested, indeed, Job was. He was suddenly stripped of his family and his wealth and finally of his health, and from a rich landowner he became a sick pauper with nothing left but his wife, who made fun of his steadfast faith in God. So Job passed the test and was rewarded with a new life, an added seventy years, a new family and doubled wealth. He still kept the same wife and so they lived happily ever after.

This was the entirely fictitious story of Job as it came to an Israelite poet whose name and date we do not know. The names are not Israelite and it may have been a foreign story. As an edifying story it suffers from the common plague of edifying stories, which is that it is so unrealistic that it becomes revolting. It is not faithful to life and it is not faithful to God. We do not believe that God plays games with human life. Only people do that. Had it not been for the Israelite poet, that sickly story would no doubt have sunk into deserved oblivion. But the poet caught the hero, who does not know what is going on, at the very bottom of his misfortunes and imagines how he might ask why everything happens to him. That celebrated question has never been so well asked.

The poet had a sense of the dramatic, although as far as we know, drama, as an art form, had not been invented. Drama means conflict and the poet secures this by introducing three of Job's friends, wealthy devout men like himself, who travel a long distance to console him.

After seven days' silence they engage in massive debate. In a stately minuet of dialogue, the poet has composed three cycles of six speeches each. In each cycle the three friends each speak once and Job responds to each. This is certainly what the poet planned. The last speeches of the third cycle have been disturbed in the manuscript tradition. The whole dialogue is introduced by a speech of Job and concluded by another speech of Job, the longest speech of all.

After this dialogue there are still ten chapters of speeches and it has long been hard for critics to believe that the author thus destroyed the balance he had been so careful to create. Most critics believe that most of the extra material was added by scribes who were not happy with what they read. They are more ready to give at least the first of the speeches of the Lord to the poet. He may have felt that since everyone has been talking about God, often quite critically, God should have a chance to speak for himself. What the scribes found wrong with the dialogue is that for a strongly devout believer, the dialogue is inconclusive; and it becomes no more conclusive if the poet added the speech of Yahweh. What I mean by the devout believer is the believer who has the belief in God which Job's friends expressed well and at length.

I have said that the story is unrealistic to the point of disgust. The poet had never known anyone who met calamity with the pious observation that the Lord gives and the Lord takes away—blessed is his name. This almost seems to refuse to take human misery seriously and it is one purpose of the poet that human misery be taken seriously. The more typical response is what the poet puts in the mouth of his hero in the translation of Marvin Pope, damn the day I was born. Why born? And if born, why not quickly dead? Such a life makes no sense. Better is a senseless death than a senseless life, for the dead feel no pain as the living do. This is the cry of mankind in inexplicable pain. The poet does not mean that all pain is inexplicable. The explicable pain causes no problem and there can be no debate unless the poet is allowed his case which is that Job is an innocent man.

But Job is not real; he is the ideal sufferer, the exemplary sufferer who represents all the unhappiness of man. It is useless to attempt to identify his disease. He has all diseases just as he has the totality of impoverishment and bereavement. He soon finds out that in addition to his other pains, he has no friends any longer.

The three friends of Job have become the classic examples of uncomfortable comforters.

The Book of Job

The classic example of the patient Job is really not in the book. After the first two chapters, Job scarcely utters a single word which could be called an expression of patience. Job's friends are wise men, and in the ancient world that title had a specialized meaning. Wisdom meant the skill of managing life, the basic skill which wise men have and fools lack. Life is well managed by doing the right things and the right things are things which wisdom teaches you to do. It is a traditional skill, rather, a set of traditional instructions handed on from father to son, from teacher to pupil. These instructions teach you how to deal with God and how to deal with men. They were, in the usual sense of the word, moral. If you follow the instructions, you cannot fail. You will succeed and prosper and live to a ripe old age. For God is the wisest of all the wise, he rewards the wise and punishes fools. To do anything else would argue that God is unwise and unjust. Job has manifestly not managed his life wisely; for what has happened to him happens only to the wicked. The comfort which his friends intend to give him is to show him why all this could not have happened to a more deserving man.

Let us be fair to Job's friends, fairer than they were to Job. The wisdom in which they believed has strong support both in the Bible and in popular belief. The Book of Deuteronomy insists to the point of weariness that the national welfare and prosperity of Israel depended on its fidelity to God's commandments. The Books of Proverbs and Psalms are full of allusions to the deserved fate of the wicked and the deserved salvation of the righteous. The whole scheme of Christian moral teaching is that God deals with men according to their works. It might be urged that the thesis of wisdom is no more than a statement, possibly somewhat crude, of a belief in providence. It is a common enough belief that the successful and prosperous have earned their success and prosperity by hard work which is a virtue and that the unsuccessful are the victims of their own indolence and lassitude, which are certainly vices. The thesis of the friends is easy to understand and is supported by more people than the poetry of the Book of Job. One can scarcely call it a thesis for it admits no neat formulation, like the thesis of wisdom. To question it seems to question God's justice and that is more or less what Job proceeds to do.

Yet once again, one is troubled by the unrealism of the story of Job. The poet, we think, did not wish to imply that there is anything like completely innocent and undeserved suffering except for infants. Such a view would be false to life and to the obvious fact that man is sinful. And it would render any discussion impossible within the framework of the wisdom in which the poet and his characters think. He does not need to go to one extreme in order to avoid the other. What the example of Job shows is that there is a lack of proportion, that good and evil in life are not apportioned to the moral worth of the individual person, that good and evil, in the words of Jesus, fall like the rain upon both the righteous and the unrighteous. If God follows a principle in apportioning good and evil, it is not the principle which the wise men assert. This, both for Job and his friends, means that there is no principle by which God apportions good and evil. And Job begins by accepting this position into which he is forced. He, too, had been a wise man and he knows the framework in which he must argue but he and his friends do not square off on equal terms. The friends have a position, a thesis, which they defend. Job has a doubt, a question. Thus, the speeches of the friends are consistent. And the poet, possibly with conscious art, permits them to become repetitious. Like so many debaters, they do not speak to the questions raised by the opposition but reaffirm and emphasize their original statement. As the cycles of discourse advance, the friends become progressively sharper in tongue and shorter in temper—again, very probably by conscious art. They begin with a fairly gentle chiding of their friend for falling into some folly from which he can escape by confession and repentance. When he insists that he has nothing to confess, they are angered because he denies an obvious theological maxim and end by screaming all sorts of charges which are manifestly false. His devout life has been a mask for concealed depravity, but God has now stripped him of pretense and shown him up for what he really is. There is, granted their principles, a certain inevitable logic in their conclusion.

The speeches of Job, on the contrary, exhibit no such consistency. He speaks to the position of his friends with hardly more directness than they show, except that he batters at their logic with the facts of experience. And the most obvious fact is himself. Experience has never been well received in debates in speculative theology and it is not well received here. Job is more of a seeker than a debater and he twists and turns trying to get out of the absurdity in which his friends' logic and his own have put him. To him the thesis of his friends is a lie in defense of God and he is sure that God does not need lies to defend himself. But he angers his friends as well as many others by saying that God does need some defense.

The poet of Job was not the first to ask this question, but there is no evidence that he knew how it had been asked by others. A Babylonian poet who may have written more than a thousand years earlier raised one possibility which our poet did not raise, the possibility that the distinction between good and evil is a purely human invention which does not at all reflect the mind of the gods. Possibly, he mused, man has it just backwards. I should add that the poet raises this possibility only to reject it, although the modern reader may wonder whether he did not, out of respect for convention, formally reject what he really believed. This is a form of moral skepticism which the poet of Job does not raise, although the questions he does raise are scarcely less shocking.

Some interpreters of the book have been fond of the word blasphemy to designate the lanuage of Job. Apart from the fact that these interpreters have left me wondering whether they know what blasphemy really is, it seems necessary to say that the language of Job does not fulfill any definition of blasphemy. He charges his friends with lying on behalf of God and he does not lie in order to raise his questions. No, he rather presents the conventional and accepted beliefs about the dealings of God with men and draws certain conclusions from them. If Job himself took part in a discussion of his blasphemies he would retort that the conventional beliefs are the blasphemies; for they compel one to say things about God which charge him with evil-doing. He might add that one who knows as little about God as his friends do must know very little about what blasphemy is.

And now let us examine some of Job's questions, fully aware that we are committing vivisection on poetry and that we kill it by reducing it to the prose of theological discourse. Nevertheless, no one has denied that the book is subtle, possibly the most subtle book of the entire Bible, and that it was difficult even for a professional Israelite wise man like its author. The modern reader may find it, as a whole, impossible, although he recognizes glimpses of great poetry and great insights at times. The modern reader may be helped if we translate the poetry into the kind of language which we use in discussing such questions. But this paraphrase is not intended to substitute for the poetry—as well substitute glucose for food. It is rather intended to help the reader to return to the poetry and share the poetic experience of the author. No commentary can ever communicate this experience.

The thesis of wisdom is unqualified optimism. It affirms that the world of human life and experience is totally rational and consistent, that its processes exhibit the sovereignly wise, good and just management of God in which each gets exactly what he deserves. I have put this in perhaps a somewhat crass formula, but it scarcely distorts the presentation, not only of Job's friends, but also of those parts of the Books of Proverbs and of Deuteronomy which express the thesis of wisdom. To say that it is not such a world is not yet to deny the attributes of God which the thesis affirms but simply to say that these attributes are not manifested in the world of experience. At this point, the skeptic might give up and say that what is not manifested in the world is not real. Job does not give up and so far escapes blasphemy.

Some of the options which Job almost frantically tosses out only to reject them deserve closer examination, for in some form most of them have found defenders in philosophy. Job suggests the hypothesis that there is a natural enmity between him and God like the natural enmity between man and beasts of prey. Job does not mean mankind at large, although the question could be extended that far. As someone once put it, is the universe friendly or hostile? But he has in view only his own personal misfortunes, which he does not see as typical. In the progress of the discourses, he comes to wonder whether misfortune is not more typical than good fortune. But the question of a natural and therefore irreconcilable enmity would remain the same. A few mythological allusions seem to indicate that the poet is thinking of the natural and perpetual enmity in creation mythology between the creative deity and the monster dragon which embodies evil and chaos. In modern terms, this would be a diabolical theory of the universe. Not God, but the devil is supreme. The first principle is not good but evil. Since Job does not generalize until later in the dialogue, the question of a diabolical universe does not arise the first time the question is asked. But it is implicit even in the question about the individual person, for it implies pure and unmotivated malice. And that is what we mean by diabolical. The word will recur, for the question of evil very quickly reduces itself to the terms of God and devil. Job rejects this theory by not pursuing it but it is in a way contained in the other options.

The theory of a supreme evil is absurd where the theory of a supreme good is only difficult. If the world were diabolical, it would be worse than it is. But it is bad and does not merely look so; we must explore other options. Another option might appear to be the theory of diabolism in another form. Perhaps God takes pleasure in destroying what he has made. He is the child who builds sand castles for the pleasure of seeing them collapse under his hand. Is the world explained on the principle that God is cruel?

Some readers have wondered whether the poet was an Israelite. I have never doubted it because the poet entertains no possibility that God is not supremely and totally powerful. Whatever happens is due to him and in no way to persons or things which he does not control. In this rather simplistic view, a tidal wave which kills 500,000 people in East Pakistan becomes a theological problem. Jesus would probably deal with this problem as he dealt with the problem of the 18 men on whom the tower fell. Unless you repent you will die the same way. It may not help to point out that the 500,000 had no business being there and the fault lies within the political and economic system which compelled them to live there. If God is all-powerful, he could have delivered them from the avarice of their exploiters as he delivered the Israelites from the Red Sea. But in normal human experience, such deliverances neither happen nor are expected to happen.

There is no question that man is cruel. The question is whether God is cruel when he does not forcibly restrain man's ferocity. Nature is never cruel, for cruelty is a human trait. But things happen in nature which look cruel to a human observer and would be cruel if they were the work of a human personal agent. The theology of omnipotence has its discomforts and the poet points out a few of them. It comes to this: that we find the appearance of cruelty more tolerable in God than the appearance of weakness. Yet again, Job rejects this form of diabolism by not pursuing it. Like the first form of diabolism it makes no sense. The supreme being cannot have a character which man is compelled to call childish or simply animal, like the child who plucks wings off insects. Here we have a key to much of the dialogue. The author can believe only in a God who measures up to human standards, low as these standards may be.

Let us turn to the hypothesis that God is simply power, pure and unmixed. This supreme power would be irrational, like the power which man perceives in nature. Indeed, the sheer power of nature is the model in most religious experience of the power of God. One cannot reason with the storm or ask it for mercy. Ancient man appealed to the personal being or beings behind the storm who could be approached in such personal terms. I said that nature is not cruel. Neither can nature be merciful. Now let us suppose that our belief in invisible personal beings is an illusion and that there is nothing there except what we can see:

pure, unreasoning, brute power—a being which is supreme simply because it is the biggest and strongest. This would be the most diabolical of all devils, surely. One is reminded of such modern writers of political nightmares as Orweli and Koestler who have created hell on earth by imagining a system by which the government is depersonalized.

One simply cannot reach non-persons. The experience of many who encounter the computer in dealing with business or government is, as they relate it, terrifying. The poet of Job is a great artist, but here it seems he did not see the depths of horror in the possibility which he opened up. In any form of the devil theory, God is seen as hostile or cruel. But when God becomes a thing, he becomes completely insensitive, not feeling even cruelty or hatred. When the supreme power is impersonal, there is no hope for the person. He may die screaming but no one is listening. This theory, too, is not pursued, even though I do believe most forms of religion and agnosticism have ultimately ended with an impersonal God who is not blind brute force only because those who think this way have not followed their logic to its full conclusions. As we have said of the other options, if this were true, the world would be worse than it is. Man thinks that he sees something which restrains that brute force which he also sees. And in that something he places his trust. Job has played with the thought that what he trusts may betray him and then laugh at him but he does not doubt that it is there. If it were brute force he could not talk to it, and that he certainly wishes to do.

There is one more option which had an even longer history in religion after Job. Let us raise the possibility that man does not know what justice is and wastes his time trying to define it or achieve it. Justice is simply what God wishes it to be. The pattern of what God does may appear to man to be a bundle of contradictions. For example, Job and his friends, as much alike as men can be, differ in their fortunes. Both cases are just for both are what God wishes them to be. There is something childish about this complaint, for the child believes that adults make up the rules as they go along. And it must be granted that they often do. Men know that they themselves make arbitrary decisions and call them justice. Job wonders whether God is really any better. He imagines himself going to court with God. He sees the opponent in the suit who is God and turns to the judge and it is God. His case is lost before it is opened. Now, can you argue at law with the one who makes the law, enforces it and adjudicates it? Against arbitrary law, Job voices what he knows to be an impossible wish, for an impartial umpire between him and God. There is no appeal from God. Yet

Job does not believe this either, although the theory that justice is what God wishes it to be won the approval of the great William of Occam, a theologian of the 14th century.

Job's complaint is not that God is artibrary in administering justice but simply that he cannot plead his case before God. What Job wants from God is simply a hearing. He is so sure of his case that he has no fear of being proved wrong. In the theology of wisdom which still dominates his thinking, God's treatment of Job is unjust and Job could prove it in a judicial process even if his accuser were his judge. But God does not communicate with man in those terms. Job cannot find his adversary. It is worth noticing that Job does not ask for the kind of solution of his case which the old story had. That did not lie within the bounds of a realistic hope. Job seems to look forward to no more than his vindication, the establishment of his innocence.

But as the dialogue advances, so does Job's perception of the problem. The later speeches of Job show a keen awareness of the length and breadth and depth of human misery. Job speaks for all who suffer. All of them need some vindication which the theology of wisdom would not allow them. The consequences of his denial of the wisdom theology do not trouble him at the moment, the consequences which might force an assertion that God does govern unjustly. The one clear perception of Job in the dialogue may be that the justice of God cannot be defended by asserting that it is realized in the world of experience. Yet Job is sure that God is just. If he is not, there is no such thing as justice and it is idle to discuss it. If God is just, he knows that the world of experience does not exhibit justice and those who say that it does tell lies about God. It is possible that the poet's insistence on the reality of suffering, both the personal suffering of Job with which the dialogue begins and the wider view of suffering in the later speeches, has the purpose of forcing the reality of the problem down the throats of those who simply do not see it.

Job's friends are typical of such. They have never suffered pain or misfortune and they are not aware that others have or of what it does to them. They themselves are at ease. If others are not, it must be their fault. How to make such people aware of the burdens of humanity has never been easy and literature, both sacred and profane, has had much to say about them. A sudden confrontation with degrading poverty or filth or disease or injury is usually too much for the stomachs of those who have led sheltered lives and certainly one of the effects of civilization is to enable as many of its citizens as possible to lead sheltered lives. The normal

The Book of Job

human reaction, as Job notices, is to avert one's face, to refuse to look upon these blemishes of the human condition. The poet of Job made a massive effort to compel the wise men of his period to look upon them. So did Jesus. The effort has to be continued.

The modern reader will no doubt ask himself whether Job considered happiness in a future life as the vindication which he sought. For the modern reader, if he is a believer, expects his own vindication in some such way, however vague the expectation may be. The closing verses of chapter 19 became, in a famous mistranslation of St. Jerome, an explicit declaration of faith in the resurrection of the body. St. Jerome engaged in guesswork because the text of these verses is so corrupt that it conveyed no meaning. It is still corrupt and modern translators confess that they are unable to extract any clear meaning from these lines. They are agreed, however, that they contain no clear allusion to the resurrection of the body and that this belief is suggested nowhere else in the book. In fact, the possibility of some form of survival after death is raised at some length in the second half of chapter 14. This would be a vindication and Job would be willing to wait for it, however long it might be delayed. But there is no hope for such a thing. The Hebrew Bible is silent about life after

John L. McKenzie

death except in two or three passages which critics place four to eight hundred years after the book of Job, which is itself of uncertain date.

The theology of wisdom dealt with personal human existence as closed by death, whatever man hoped or feared he would experience between birth and death. Clearly, this lent weight to the wisdom theology. If one chance is all man gets, God owes him a fair chance. On the other, the modern reader may think that his belief in life after death solves the problem of evil. It does not. It merely allows God to save his reputation by postponing justice. We do not apply to God the saying that justice delayed is justice denied. Nor do we face the evident truth that what God can do later he can do now. The question raised by the poet of Job is still urgent and still unanswered. As we have remarked earlier, the theology of omnipotence has its discomforts.

It should be admitted, it seems, that the theology of heaven and hell, which must be carefully distinguished from belief in life after death, have often prevented Christians from feeling pressure on themselves to lighten the load of human misery. They forget that Jesus spoke much more frequently and much more seriously about lightening the burden of human misery than he did about the resurrection of the

The Book of Job

body. The dialogue of the book of Job, we have noticed, is inconclusive. The closing speech of Job is a long profession of his innocence. He has stated his case. Now he challenges God to state his charge. If he did, Job is sure that he could wear the indictment as a badge of honor. The debate has come to a standstill. No one doubts that the author meant to confute the theology of wisdom, but he has not solved the problem which he has raised.

But it seems fitting and proper that God should have an opportunity to speak. He has been challenged often enough. The dialogue has perhaps shown nothing except that wisdom is bankrupt in the presence of massive evil. It has no skill in life management which can cope with calamity. Can God, who sends and withholds calamity, speak to this thing which turns wisdom into folly? God does speak, although most critics who think his speech belongs to the poem believe that it was expanded by one or two enthusiastic imitators who were carried away by the paradoxes of the hippopotamus and the crocodile. But God does not answer Job nor does he rebuke him for intemperate language. The rebuke is given for talking about things he does not understand.

Creation is presented as a collection of paradoxes which man could not think up and

115

could not manage if he did think of them. Some of the paradoxes are presented in a somewhat simplistic view of nature. The ostrich is really not a cruel mother. But the modern sophisticated view of nature has scarcely rendered it less paradoxical; in spite of the paradoxes or rather through them the world continues to move and to sustain life. This is presented as the attestation of the wisdom of God. He manages the world in mysterious ways which surpass Job's understanding. The implied conclusion is that the management of the world of human life, which is a supreme paradox in all creation, is even more mysterious and demands even greater wisdom. It is not even a challenge to set forth a better way of doing it, if you know a better way. It is not a simple assertion of power. It is rather a demand that Job accept the world as it is and God as he is, even if he does not understand either. It is, in a rather peculiar and roundabout way, a challenge to faith.

At the risk of being more subtle than the author, I think he meant to say that the faith that will carry one through such a crisis as the crisis of Job is not possible without religious experience, an experience of God which gives one a new insight into the reality of God which is not conveyed by conventional wisdom in any age. Job has been granted such an experience. It may come as a disappointment to the reader of the dialogue because it does not convey to him the insight which it did to the author.

The reader may be looking for an answer to the speculative problem of evil and the poet had no answer to this. In fact, no one has given an answer to the speculative problem, not even Jesus. What the poet believed he had found and what Jesus proposed was not an answer to the problem of evil, but a way in which one can live with it. Rarely does one meet a man or a woman who has learned how to live at peace with evil. When one does meet such a person, one knows that one has encountered wisdom which recognizes God in the world as it is

Isaiah

SINCE 1789, scholars have called the last 27 chapters of the Book of Isaiah by the name of Second Isiah or, lapsing into Greek, Deutero-Isaiah. Since 1892, they have further separated chapters 56 through 66 from Second Isaiah and called them Third Isaiah, or Trito-Isaiah. First Isaiah, or Isaiah of Jerusalem, is dated from 740 to 700 B.C. Second Isaiah is dated 550 to 545 B.C. Third Isaiah, a collection of assorted anonymous works, is dated 500 to 450 B.C. Those who object to this critical dissection of a book which has been called Isaiah since the 2nd century before Christ must simply not have read seriously much less closely the book in question.

If Isaiah 40 through 55 were left without any name and given to scholars to guess its date, they would be compelled to give it a date near 550 B.C. They would reach this conclusion by a study of the contents of the book, what it tells us about contemporary history and the situation of the people whom it addresses. They would present very persuasive reasons based on style and vocabulary that it is the work of a different author from most of the first 39 chapters, to speak with proper caution. How Second and Third Isaiah were ever joined to First Isaiah is a legitimate question and scholars would be happier if they knew the answer. But they have long been convinced the thought processes of ancient scribes often elude the analysis of modern learning. The data and the situation of Isaiah 40 through 55 are possibly the most assured conclusions of modern biblical criticism. Since it seems possible to give the book a fairly precise location and date, some understanding of the situation in which it was composed should make it easier to understand the book itself.

In the year 587 B.C., the kingdom of Judah and the city of Jerusalem were destroyed by the Babylonian army commanded by the greatest king of Babylon, Nebuchadnezzar. How this happened is less important for the understanding of the book than the fact that the end of the kingdom of Judah was as total and final as the end of any of the other petty kingdoms of the ancient near east which perished in the conquests of the Assyrian and the Babylonian Empires. Indeed, Assyria itself, a greater power than Babylon, disappeared without a trace in the same series of wars which brought an end to the kingdom of Judah.

Jerusalem and the major cities of Judah were reduced to ruins and a large proportion of the population, numbering in the thousands, were removed from the country and settled in the Babylonian Empire. This community of exile was addressed by the anonymous prophet whom we know as Second Isaiah. It is evident from the text that he spoke to a group uprooted from their homeland. The exiled group of Judahites were swept into the current of world history.

The rise of the Persian Empire was contemporaneous with the peak of the Babylonian Empire. Under the aggressive rule of Cyrus the Great, the Persian Empire reached a degree of power at which it was able to overturn the Babylonian Empire, weakened after the death of Nebuchadnezzar, in 562 B.C. The overturn was accomplished by the conquest of Babylon in 539 B.C. In 537 B.C. Cyrus invited those Jews who wished to return to their own land to resettle Jerusalem and Palestine. This was done as soon as possible and the Jewish community under Persian imperial rule was established. Cyrus did nothing during his reign which had more lasting results in world history.

Second Isaiah addressed to the Jews in Babylonia a message of hope and promise. He knows Cyrus of Persia by name and greets him as the savior promised by God. He goes so far as to greet Cyrus by titles traditionally given to the messianic king of Judah. The text suggests that he wrote after Cyrus had become powerful enough to pose a real threat to Babylonian supremacy but before the actual conquest of Babylon. The decade 550 to 540 B.C. suits these writings with astonishing precision, and even more closely, the years 546, when Cyrus conquered the kingdom of Lydia in Asia Minor, to 540.

The reader of Second Isaiah must attempt to reconstruct in imagination the hopelessness of the people to whom the prophet spoke. Only those who have experienced a similar catastrophe can realize the totality of the defeat of the kingdom of Judah in 587 B.C. There was no more reason to think that a new Judah would arise from the ruins of war than there was to expect the resurrection of any other of the petty kingdoms of the ancient near east which had been swallowed up by the military machines of Assyria and Babylonia. In fact, none of these other kingdoms did return to political life. We do not understand either Second Isaiah or his readers if we think that they had any hope of survival when he addressed them. Political realism would not allow any such fantastic hopes to arise. Judah was, to all purposes, politically dead, the dry bones of the vision of Ezekiel, chapter 37. Yet to this people Second Isaiah addressed his message of hope and promise in such eloquent and exalted language that the Christian church for centuries has used his words generously in the liturgy of advent to announce the coming of a saving event which sound interpretation forbids us to think was intended by Second Isaiah.

It is necessary to set forth as clearly as possible what the content and meaning of this hope and promise were. Through the centuries since Second Isaiah wrote, the prophet has been often enough misunderstood and misapplied so that his message has been trivialized and secularized. The application of his message to the coming of Christ is in itself a relatively harmless misinterpretation. But some of the figures of his poetic speech have been applied to events with less innocent consequences.

The first element in the promise is that there will be a future for this people. And the question of what this people is to be called needs some explanation. The historical and religious name for the people of the Old Testament is Israel. In the 10th century B.C., the people of Israel were divided into two kingdoms, the larger of which retained the name of Israel and the smaller took the name of the tribe of Judah. The kingdom of Judah was ruled by the dynasty of David which had its seat in the city of Jerusalem. The kingdom of Israel was destroyed by the Assyrians in the 8th century B.C. and the kingdom of Judah preserved the religion and the traditions of Israel. Second Isaiah addressed his people as Jacob or Israel, recalling the earliest traditions of the people, or as Zion, recalling the most recent form in which the people of Israel had existed. In any case, the designations of the people recalled the God whom Israel had worshipped in its beginning and throughout its history, the God who had inflicted a total judgment on his people for their infidelity to him. That Israel should have a future will demand and act of God as mighty as the act which had summoned Israel into existence. Second Isaiah presents this saving act as another exodus and another march through the desert. It is entirely an act of God. Israel does nothing. It experiences the saving power and will of God.

We have noticed that political realism did not allow fantastic hopes. Second Isaiah does not promise that Israel will deliver itself by arms or diplomacy. It must await the act of God and it cannot even choose the instruments of deliverance. Apparently, Second Isaiah had listeners who found it hard to believe that God would save his people through a heathen conqueror. The paradox of salvation was not rendered more credible by the fact that the manner of salvation was also incredible.

Did God need the heathen whom he had not needed in the exodus? The future which Second Isaiah promises for his people is not a political future. If he had found reasons why the God of all the world should have chosen to preserve this one political group while he let others vanish into oblivion, he would have presented theological problems which we would be unable to answer. Israel is returned to life, not for political purposes but because God chooses to employ this people for purposes which cannot be achieved by political means.

Strictly speaking, not even this people is necessary to the purpose which God, as Second Isaiah speaks for him, is supposed to have. It is essential to Christian belief that the purposes for which God revived Israel were later transferred to the new Israel, the church of Christ. This is the basic issue which divides Jews from Christians. But Jews and Christians must agree that the purpose was not political. The new exodus did not occur in order that a new member of the political community might arise. For that, God is not necessary. Thus, Second Isaiah does not promise a restoration of the monarchy or of the empire of David. Why should a proved failure be reenacted? He does not even promise a restoration of the temple. This is mentioned in only one passage which may have been added by a commentator.

There are some grandiose promises about a New Jerusalem. It seems that these must be read in the light of the place defined for the New

Israel in history. Israel is not resuscitated in order to be one political or ethnic community among many but in order to fulfill a mission. The qualification of Israel for the mission is rooted in the history of Israel, for Israel alone among all peoples knows God.

The word know is used here with the peculiar implications of the Hebrew word which we translate as know. Israel alone has heard God speak and seen him act. Israel alone has had the experience of God as a personal reality. Israel alone has the experience which it can communicate to others who have not so known God. Israel is like the one who has had a personal conversation with a great man, like the traveler who has visited famous sights and famous cities. What Israel can tell cannot be learned from mere reading and study. Hence, Israel is equipped for the mission as no other people is.

The mission is to make God known to other peoples. No biblical writer before Second Isaiah stated so clearly that Israel worshipped the one God of all mankind. No other writer stated that Israel existed, that it had been created by God in order to be his representative and his spokesman to other nations. There is, of course, an implicit idea of fellowship in the mission which was not fully stated by Second Isaiah. It is much that the idea is present in germ. The earlier books of the Old Testament show no

Isaiah

profound awareness of the fellowship of men under one God. Not infrequently they give expression to the kind of political and ethnic prejudice which we know too well. Second Isaiah introduced something quite new into his community and it appears that he was aware of it. It was no longer possible to think that God had one purpose for his chosen people and no purpose for all others. In fact, the very idea of chosen people was so radically changed by the theme of mission that it was no longer meaningful.

The prophet Amos, 200 years earlier, had attempted another revision of the idea: "You alone have I known among all the other peoples of the world, therefore I will punish you." The position of Zion in the message now becomes clearer, although there are still obscurities. We do not understand the link which unites a people with its land, the link which gives the people an identity. But we can see that in Second Isaiah the nations stream to Jerusalem in submission, not as to an imperial center but as to the place from which they have learned the worship of the one true God. Second Isaiah apparently never saw the political possibilities of such a center of religion. Others have seen them. The wealth which flows to Jerusalem is not the wealth looted by conquest but the wealth of generous offerings in sacrifice, for Jerusalem will be the cultic center of the world. The vision of Second Isaiah did not extend to a future in which men should not worship God on this or that mountain, but in spirit and in truth. It is clear that the leadership of Israel over the nations is the leadership exercised by a prophet over those to whom he proclaims God.

The God whom Israel proclaims to the nations is revealed in his true character in the history of Israel. He is revealed as righteous, a God who insists upon obedience to his will. Israel is a witness to his judgments upon the unrighteous. Even the people whom he has chosen is not spared the full measure of justice for wrongdoing. But if he is a righteous God, he is also a God of mercy and forgiveness. The very existence of a restored Israel is the witness to these attributes. The restored Israel must turn from the wickedness of the past to obedience to the way of God. Harmony with God does not depend on ritual observance alone nor is it imperiled by the caprice of an all-powerful but sometimes irrational deity. The ancient world knew both of these obstacles to genuine religion. Harmony with God is secured by acceptance of his moral will which he makes known clearly to those who profess to believe in him.

There are two prominent themes in Second Isaiah which are less prominent or even totally absent in earlier writings. And the modern interpreters have asked to what extent these may have been original with Second Isaiah. To modern believers these two themes are well known as basic. And they may be surprised to learn that in the earlier development of biblical religion, these themes were not as readily taken for granted as they are by us.

The first of these themes is monotheism, the doctrine that there is one and only one God. The ancient near east was a world of polytheism, and students of the Bible have often been puzzled by the fact that polemic in defense of monotheism is not more frequent in the earlier books of the Old Testament. We have not yet fully reconstructed the belief of the earlier Israelites. It did not take the form of doctrinal statements and creeds such as ours but found its fullest expression in cultic worship. There is nothing in the background of the earlier books to explain why Second Isaiah becomes a militant spokesman for monotheism.

Students of the Bible reflect that the total defeat of Judah was also, to all appearances, a total defeat for the God of Israel. Ancient deities did not survive the total defeat of their peoples. But if the God of Israel is the one and only God of all peoples, he is neither victorious nor defeated in the rise and fall of nations. His victories, as in the history of Israel, are seen in his assertion of his moral imperatives in the rise and fall of nations. His moral supremacy is seen in the fall of Judah, as interpreted by Israelite prophets, and in the fall of Babylon, as announced by Second Isaiah. The gods of Babylon could not protect their city because they are unreal. The god of Judah did not protect his people because they had forfeited any claim to his protection. The reality of his power can be seen in his effective decision to restore the people of Judah as his witnesses. Certainly the people of Judah must have been moved to doubts about their God as they had never been moved before. Not only had he failed to defend them against the armies of Babylon (after all the prophets had explained why this had happened to any who cared to listen), but now they had seen and experienced at first hand the wealth and magnificence of these peoples who worshipped nonexistent gods. Any one of the numerous temples of Babylon made their ruined temple of Jerusalem look like a wayside shrine. The wealth of nations which Second Isaiah announced would flow to Jerusalem actually flowed into Babylon. And the nations were its subjects and slaves. Second Isaiah had to convince his people that wealth and power were not demonstrations that the gods of Babylon were successful. Moral purity has never been a very persuasive argument against such manifestations of control of the forces of nature and of history.

The second of the themes to which Second Isaiah gives a new prominence is creation. It is now known that the religions of the ancient near east were dominated by the cosmic myth of creation in which the production of the world by the creator god was the result of a victory over the monster of chaos. The myth reflected the cycle of life and death; the victory of the creator god was followed by his own death in combat with the monster of chaos. Thus, creation was not an event with which the world and time begin but an annually recurring alteration of life and death in which neither life nor death is finally victorious. Second Isaiah may have been the first biblical writer to see that this myth failed to acknowledge the supremacy of the one and only God whom he proclaimed. There are reasons for thinking that early Israel simply transferred the myth of the creative combat to their own God without reflection on its implications. Certainly the myth left abundant traces in biblical literature, even in Second Isaiah. Yet it is clear that to Second Isaiah, creation is a single event, not a recurring struggle, and that this one event manifests the cosmic power of the one only God as nothing else does. The Judahites should readily place their faith and hope in the one God whose power produced the whole visible universe, to whom everything in that universe is subject and who has no rival power with which he must compete.

Included in the text of Second Isaiah are four short poems identified since 1892 as the poems of the servant of the Lord. These poems appear in chapter 42, verses one through 4; chapter 49, verses one through 6; chapter 50, verses 4 through 9; chapter 52, verse 13, through chapter 53, verse 12. The reader can easily see that the four poems stand isolated in the context. While they do not form a single poem when taken together, they have a community of theme and style. The servant of the Lord is a speaker in the second and third poems. He is the topic of the poem in the first and fourth. The first three poems are followed by a response in chapter 42, verses 5 through 9; chapter 49, verses 7 through 13 and chapter 50, verses 10 through 11. It has recently been propsed that chapter 53, verses 10 through 12, is a response to the fourth poem. The responses are the work of a different hand from the author of the poems. No single passage of the Bible has created so many problems for scholars as the servant poems. If the reader finds them difficult to understand, he is on the right track. Most modern scholars believe they are not the work of Second Isaiah and have been inserted into his work. Why they were inserted at these points is not understood. The reader who finds that they are foreign to the context assesses them quite correctly. The responses as well as the poems are attributed to still another writer, as we have noticed, who is also later than Second Isaiah.

The major and still unsolved problem in the servant poems is the identity of the servant. And nearly every possible identification has been suggested, only to be later abandoned. If the servant is said to be a historical figure, the interpretation is meaningless unless the figure can be identified. Efforts to do this have failed. If he is not historical, he must be an imaginary or ideal figure created by the prophet. In this hypothesis, there is a vagueness about the character which permits interpreters to dispute about the precise meaning of the figure.

Two ancient and venerated interpretations are generally rejected by modern scholars. The first of these is that the servant is an ideal figure who represents the people of Israel. While some latitude must be allowed a poet in the creation of ideal figures, the servant, who seems in the fourth poem to undergo a death which atones for others, is entirely alien, not only to Israel as viewed generally in the prophets, but as viewed in the second and third parts of the Book of Isaiah.

John L. McKenzie

Other features of the servant can be combined with the idea of Israel as a witness discussed above. In some ways the servant, while he is not Israel, appears to represent Israel. The second interpretation is the identification of the servant with Jesus Christ. This view is supported by the fact that the New Testament sometimes uses the figure of servant to define the saving role of Jesus. To use the servant as a model to describe the role of Jesus, however, is not the same thing as to say that the servant predicted the preaching, the passion and the atoning death of Jesus. That type of prediction, modern scholars believe, is not found in Old Testament prophecy. They know that when they say this they take a stand in opposition to several hundred years of Christian biblical interpretation. It can be suggested that the servant is set up as a savior pattern in opposition to the king savior reflected often in the Old Testament.

We have observed that Second Isaiah sees no politics in the future missionary role of Israel. Yet Israel as the revealer of God has a saving role to play towards the nations. How is this saving role to be accomplished? The poems sketch its elements. In the first poem the servant appears as another Moses who reveals God's teaching to the nations. In the second poem the servant is a light, both to the nations and to

Isaiah

Israel. Light, in biblical language, is less a symbol of knowledge or understanding than of deliverance and salvation. The third poem sees the servant accomplishing his mission in spite of opposition. The fourth poem sees the servant as saving others through his own suffering and death. We have here, it seems, isolated fragments of a vision which the poet never put together. It is derived from the ideas of Moses as teacher and revealer and from the idea of the prophet as a spokesman for God. The idea of vicarious atonement is really without parallel in the Old Testament. The vision of the prophet was so novel, so foreign both to his own experience and to the experience of those to whom he spoke, that we should not be surprised at his failure to put the elements together. We can see, it seems, that he wishes to move away from any idea that the future of Israel is to be a victory of Israel over the nations and the establishment of a world empire by the power of God, over which Israel should rule. That such political hopes were fostered in the world of Second Isaiah and after him is evident from many passages of the Bible. The belief that man was to be saved by atoning, suffering and death was foreign to men of the 6th century B.C. It is still foreign to many believers.

It appears that the study of Second Isaiah is a clear instance of a book where the work of

John L. McKenzie

modern biblical criticism has made a depth of understanding possible which could not be reached when the book was regarded as the product of a writer 200 years earlier. We have learned the situation to which this prophet addressed himself. As always in the Bible, we hear the speakers most clearly when we hear them speak to the audience which they really addressed. That much of what they said to that audience is meaningful to us rests on the fact that we and that community share certain problems and hopes.

War and Peace in the New Testament

THE New Testament knows no wars in which Christians engage except the war of the flesh against the spirit and the war of the world and the demons against the church. Only in the second of these wars could there be any thought of conflict in the usual sense of the term—military conflict. But the New Testament warns Christians to deal with the world as its victims, not as its military opponents. The victory of the Christian over the world is to be achieved in the same way in which Jesus achieved his victory, by the death of the Christian. Consequently, the New Testament gives no directions at all on how the Christian is to conduct himself in war.

The New Testament does not see Christians engaged in war. One may indeed refer to the words attributed to John the Baptist addressed to Roman soldiers in Palestine. He told them to wrong no man and to be content with their pay. This second recommendation, unrealistic in the modern economy, really means that the soldiers should not make up what they believe was lacking in their pay by extortion from the people whom they policed. Outside of this, which is not addressed to Christians engaged in military service, nothing is found at all. On only one occasion in the life of Jesus did the question of armed defense arise. This was the occasion of his arrest in Gethsemane. Armed defense in such a situation is hardly parallel to war but the ethics of self-defense and the ethics of war in Christian theology have been substantially the same. The meagre defense which the disciples were ready to attempt against the arresting force was refused by Jesus and refused rather sharply. In the gospel of Matthew, the refusal is expanded by saying that those who take the sword shall perish by the sword. This saying is not found in the other gospels. As far as Christian interest in the saying is concerned, it might just as well not have been found in Matthew. The arrest is not necessarily the original context of this saying. But the evangelist has achieved a certain dramatic contrast by placing the saying in a context where anyone would believe that legitimate self-defense was in place if it ever was.

In the same gospel of Matthew we find the fullest exposition of the Christian ethic of nonresistance. This is found in the Sermon on the Mount and, as one reads the verses which deal with nonresistance, one must admit that they are in no way qualified by the hypothesis of situations in which they would not be in place. If

War and Peace in the New Testament

Christian interpreters add qualifications to this statement, they would not be doing anything that they have not done elsewhere in the gospels. At the same time, the reader may sometimes wonder why it has been so easy to qualify the ethic of nonresistance and so difficult to qualify the ethic of divorce and remarriage. Were the principles by which nonresistance has been rendered nugatory in the Christian ethic applied to the principles of divorce and remarriage the Catholic church would be as ready to admit divorced and remarried persons to communion as any other Christian church. The reasons for this are too far to seek in this brief exposition. But one who believes in fidelity to the very words of Jesus can afford to consider whether his fidelity is equally present in all the words of Jesus.

Much of Christian moral teaching and moral tradition have been concerned with finding and explaining exceptions to the ethic of non-resistance for the individual person and for the state. For the individual person, legitimate self-defense is a commonplace in the Christian moral theology. Moral theologians do not forbid the individual Christian to refuse resistance. This would be in such evident opposition to the words of the gospel that even moral theologians can see it. But they admit no situation in which nonresistance is obligatory. This has meant effectively that the words of Jesus on nonresistance have had practically no moral impact on Christian moral teaching and only rare and occasional impacts in the life of individual Christians who have come to believe somehow that the words of Jesus should be taken more seriously than they have been in traditional Christian moral teachings.

Such instances have always been isolated. Had the effort been made to explain, to justify, and to teach the ethic of nonresistance which has been expended on explaining the righteousness of legitimate self-defense, one believes that the Christians might have found the ethic of nonresistance less unreal than they are accustomed to believe that it is. These words of Jesus in common belief and in common speech express an impossible ideal towards which the Christian community moves with no hope that it will ever be attained. The Christian community since the first three centuries has never been a community of nonresistance and nothing in its present situation indicates that is is going to become such a community now.

The ethic of the individual person and the ethic of the state are not entirely the same where the use of force is concerned. In civilized communities there is a political authority which forbids the individual person to use force except in the hypothesis of legitimate self-defense. In our own laws, even this hypothesis cannot be assumed but must be proved in the legal process. There is no political authority above the state. There is no superior authority which can forbid the state to use force when the state believes that force is the only method by which its ends can be achieved or even when the state believes that force is the best method by which its ends can be achieved.

In Christian moral teaching the ethic of the person is not transferred to the ethic of the state. The state lives under a different moral system from the moral system which governs the lives of its citizens as individual persons. Again, much of Christian moral teaching has been dedicated to establishing the ethic of the state and in particular, the ethic of the state's use of force. This has meant that the church has normally, during most of its history, proclaimed the ethic of the just war instead of the ethic of nonresistance. The ethic of the just war corresponds somewhat to the ethic of legitimate self-defense for the individual person. The ethic of the just war, for instance, has never justified what is called aggressive war. Yet theoretical thinkers have never hesitated to say that denial of aggressive war does not of necessity mean denial of the first military move. In the world of politics we are ready to conceive that the first move may be made as legitimate response to an

John L. McKenzie

aggressive movement which the adversary has not yet made but which he is reasonably expected to make. This kind of ethical thinking has gone through the entire structure of just war ethics.

In the last analysis, one wonders whether any war has ever been fought by any nation which could be called a just war in the sense that it has met all the conditions of the just war which moral theologians lay down. No such war is known to me. And I should be glad to hear of one. Yet, according to the principles of the just war and according to the general principles of moral theology, an action which is partially bad becomes an action which is morally impossible. If the war cannot be conducted without violation of justice, moral theologians will not admit it. The fact that they have defended certain wars in which Christian nations have engaged would seem to show that they do not know very much about the way in which wars are conducted.

Much of the discussion of the ethics of the just war reminds the student of the celebrated medieval discussion about the number of angels who can dance on the point of a needle. The discussions had nothing to do with the realities of war. One does not know whether this failure to touch reality was due entirely to the scholar's ignorance of the realities of war, an ignorance which I and the scholars share, or whether it

142

was due to a deliberate refusal to study these realities in the ways in which scholars can study them. We are again confronted with the fact that Christian theologians have expended an enormous amount of time and effort in studying something other than the New Testament.

The New Testament says nothing about the just war. This does not imply that there can be no ethic of the just war. Modern civilization raises a number of moral problems which are not expressly dealt with in the New Testament. The questions raised by the ethics of the just war are, however, questions about reconciling these ethics with the words attributed to Jesus himself on the use of violence between men. Some of us find it impossible to reconcile the two. We are ready to admit that both Christian theory and Christian practice have found it impossible to live with the words attributed to Jesus. This has meant historically that effectively Jesus said nothing about nonresistance. What he did say has been found impossible to practice. Yet, when one examines the words, one sees that quite simply the recommendation of Jesus for the achievement of peace is that one of the contending parties should stop fighting.

The ethics of the just war, instead, permit us to continue fighting until one of the contending parties is no longer able to contend. It excuses both the contending parties from ending hostilities as long as the other party does not end hostilities first. Obviously, we are faced here with a logical as well as a practical impossibility. And it is not surprising then, that during most of the history of Christianity, most Christian nations have most of the time been engaged in warfares, all of which were unjust. What else could be expected? War is indeed a curse but it is a curse which men would rather have than peace. No effective program of peace has been presented except the ethic of nonresistance.

I wish not to limit our attention to those words of the New Testament which deal directly with violence and its denunciation. I would rather see attention drawn to the fact that in most of the books of the New Testament reconciliation has a primary place in the mission and the ethic of the church, and in the mission and the ethic of the individual Christian. The church as a group and the individual Christian as a person within his own social group are supposed to be agents of peace, which means that they reconcile. The basic reconciliation which the New Testament looks toward and the reconciliation which most of us hope to see realized is reconciliation of man with God. The New Testament often concedes man's position before God as a position of enmity. God is ready to forgive. God is open to reconciliation. He himself has initiated reconciliation through the death of his son who is the great reconciler. Man really has very little to do except submit himself to the offer.

Yet there is more to reconciliation with God than simple repentance in the sense of regret for one's misdeeds. An express condition which Jesus himself lays down for reconciliation of man to God is reconciliation of men with each other. Again, in the gospel of Matthew, the duty of reconciliation is given a priority over the duty of worship, that religious duty which in the minds of most people is absolutely first. This is not the teaching of Jesus. If our brother has something against us, we should leave the gift where we are and go first to be reconciled before we go to worship. This saying of Jesus has been treated with the same degree of practical realism in the Christian community as the saying about nonresistance. The Christians have learned long ago, and know well now, that worship can be a religious duty which makes almost no demands on one. This was clear to the prophets of the Old Testament. Where Isaiah spoke in his day of trampling in the courts of Yahweh, one wonders whether in modern times he might not speak of trampling in the modern church or in the cathedral.

Is God pleased with us? Jesus tells us he is not pleased unless men have first become reconciled with each other. And the saying does not lay the blame for the difference on either one of the parties. The Christian who hears the message is directed to make the move towards reconciliation. No consideration is given as to whether he is the offender or the offended. I may add that in much of conventional moral theology one is excused from reconciliation in many situations in which one is the offended. In reconciliation, as in nonviolence or nonresistance, the first move is laid upon the Christian and not upon the other party, whoever the other party may be. The ideal which is placed before the world in these words is that peace which is achieved by universal reconciliation. Like nonresistance, it is regarded as an ideal which is not practical. Yet I do not believe anyone would deny that a genuine peace is not achieved without reconciliation. I do not believe that anyone could deny that reconciliation does not mean peace with victory. The Christian, if he follows the teachings of Jesus, achieves peace by yielding, not by conquering.

One may say of this what is said of another saying of Jesus elsewhere in the gospels: this is a hard saying if you can believe it. In fact, very few have believed it. We have found it too hard to live with, too hard to execute. What is remarkable is the serenity with which so many Christians quite freely select the words of Jesus which they will follow and reject those with which they cannot live and still proclaim to their fellow believers and to the unbelieving world that they are with Christ. The gospel word for such is heresy.

One may add a learned note to this summary of New Testament teaching, a note which is not drawn precisely from the New Testament. It seems worth our notice that the Christian ethic of nonresistance and of reconciliation has been observed by the Christian body only during the first three centuries of the history of the church. One may observe that the Christians during the first three centuries of the church were a politically helpless and inactive group. They were in no position to take political or military action against the Roman empire. And I may add another note parenthetically: the amount of persecution which the Roman government effectively inflicted on the early Christian church has been exaggerated in Christian legend. Two or three genuinely serious efforts were made to destroy the Christian community. A German scholar, now deceased, said several years ago that only a few Roman officers and a few Christians had the insight to see that the Roman empire could not survive if it were conquered by the Christian ethic, meaning the Christian ethic of nonresistance and nonviolence. Those emperors who perceived this attempted to destroy what they felt would destroy the Roman empire.

John L. McKenzie

In fact, their suspicions were verified. The Roman empire did become Christian and the conquest of the Roman empire by Christianity was achieved through nonresistance and reconciliation. It was the most effective Christian movement against a government which has ever been made.

At the same time, the victory was scarcely complete. In fact, one may call it a fallacious victory. It is true that the empire became Christian. It is also true that the church became Roman. And once the church became Roman and the empire became Christian, the ethic of nonresistance and nonviolence gave place to the Roman ethic of war and conquest. The church blessed the means for conquest as soon as it had these means available. And one wonders whether the church will cease to bless them only when they are no longer available.

I said that the ethic of the just war permits the state to be the only and supreme ultimate judge of whether force is the best means or a good means to achieve its ends. This was the ethic of the Roman empire, which was not totally barbarous, not totally cruel, and not totally ineffective as an agency of government of millions of people. It viewed force simply for its political values. No ethics were involved. No one had ever suggested that they should be involved. The church did suggest it but ultimately yielded to the Roman ethic. It has never changed its position on this since. This means that as a political activity the church really no longer believes in martyrdom.

The word martyr means, of course, witness. One witnesses to the truth of what he believes by preferring death to changing his mind. Martyrdom is not something to be easily or quickly recommended. According to all reports, it is a rather difficult test of character. Yet the church boasts of its martyrs. The church has expressed its belief in words attributed to Tertullian, a citizen of the Roman Empire, that the blood of martyrs is the seed of Christians. The sincerity of the witness attested unto death is impressive. It does move people to believe that the teaching of Jesus is the truth and the life. But if sufficient force is available, who needs martyrs? People will believe in Jesus, not because they believe that in him is life and truth but because the believers will do them a great deal of harm if they refuse to believe. This is not, indeed, to say that the modern church embarks on crusades. Yet the word has been used and too many prelates of distinction have blessed the use of force rather than nonresistance and reconciliation. In this respect we may ask whether what we proclaim is really the gospel of our Lord and savior, Jesus Christ.

Evaluating the Deluge Myth

CONTEMPORARY biblical studies carried on by Catholic scholars have excited considerable interest within the Catholic community, interest which is both flattering and hostile. Catholic scholars are convinced that they are doing no more than executing the mandate which Pius XII gave them in the encyclical *Divino Afflante Spiritu* of 1943. The scrutiny to which their work has been subjected has disclosed nothing in the biblical movement as a whole which can be defined as a deviation from the mandate.

Popular interest in biblical studies has usually been centered on the *conclusions* of the scholars rather than on their methods, for the good reason that acquaintance with the methods of biblical studies can be gained only by prolonged and assiduous application to these studies. But of late, interest has more and more turned to the methods; Catholics would like to have a clearer idea of how scholars arrive at their conclusions. This chapter is intended to be a sample of methods as applied to a question now regarded as closed in modern interpretation: the story of the deluge. Because it is closed, no doubts should arise about the use of the methods here. And where the methods have been proved valid, it is legitimate to extend them to other problems which admit the same type of analysis. Obviously it cannot be determined whether these other problems admit the same analysis until the analysis is attempted.

That the deluge, related in Genesis 6-9, was a historical event narrated exactly as it happened was not questioned until the nineteenth century. To say that it could not have been questioned may be too much. We can now see how the question could have been raised; this does not imply that earlier scholars ought to have raised it. The acceptance of the spherical shape of the earth and the knowledge of its vast dimensions led some interpreters to question whether the deluge was properly universal; but with this reservation the historical character of the account was not otherwise seriously doubted.

What reasons now appear for raising the question? One is the obvious assumption that the story of the deluge, like the other elements of Genesis 1-11, presents a condition of man altogether different from the known conditions of historic man. In other collections of folklore the creation of an imaginary world so different from the world of experience is clear evidence that we deal with something other than history.

Evaluating the Deluge Myth

But it was assumed without question that biblical narrative never deals with things other than history, that fiction of any kind is beneath the dignity of God and of the Bible, the word of God. If this faith in biblical history compelled one to assume the existence of an unrealistic world, then the assumption was accepted. Biblical discourse moved in the biblical universe, and both were subject to their own laws. One left the world of experience when one entered the world of the Bible. In the world of the Bible anything could happen.

Very few protests against this position were heard before the nineteenth century; and those who did protest hurt their position by the manner and tone of their protests. Like the orthodox, they thought that fictitious narrative was unworthy of the Bible; and they uttered their doubts as a part of a denial of the historical and religious value of the Bible. They were incapable of attaching any value other than the historical to the deluge story. Consequently, their protests were rightly stigmatized as "rationalism," and the Christian churches, both Catholic and Protestant, refused to take account of the protests. It was still too early to consider the deluge story for its theological significance.

What turned the direction of interpretation

was the discovery of the Mesopotamian deluge story. This story is found in the XI tablet of the Epic of Gilgamesh, discovered in the vast library collected at Nineveh by Ashurbanipal, king of Assyria, 668-630 B.C. Other fragments of the epic show that the Akkadian form of the poem is at least as old as the Old Babylonian period, the first part of the second millennium B.C. In 1914, a fragment of the Sumerian form of the poem, which shows that the poem existed in the third millennium B.C., was published. In the Akkadian form, the hero of the poem, Gilgamesh, journeys to the ends of the earth in search of the plant of life, and there he encounters Ut-napishtim, who with his wife has survived the deluge and is granted immortality by the gods. The story as told in answer to the request of Gilgamesh relates that Enlil became angry with man and was determined to destroy him; but Ut-napishtim was forewarned by the god Ea, who favored him. At Ea's instructions he built a huge boat with seven decks, into which he took his family and animals and craftsmen, lest the crafts perish. After a rain of a week's duration which brought total inundation, the boat finally came to rest on a mountain. Ut-napishtim sent out a dove, a swallow and a raven to find whether the waters had run off. He then came forth and offered sacrifice, at which the gods assembled.

Evaluating the Deluge Myth

When Enlil found that Ut-napishtim had escaped, he was angered. But Ea charged him with excess; he should have sent a lesser agent of his anger such as a wild beast, famine or pestilence.

It was evident when the Gilgamesh epic was deciphered and translated, that the epic and Genesis 6-9 related the same story. It was equally evident that the Mesopotamian deluge story was of earlier origin than the Genesis account; in any hypothesis of Israelite origins, the deluge story was written long before any group called Israel came into existence. If there is any literary dependence, it is dependence of Israel on Mesopotamia. And literary dependence there must be; if it does not exist here, it exists nowhere. The dependence is shown by much more than the common account of a deluge in which one family escapes by the construction of a barge. It appears in little details like the animals of the ark and the use of the birds to ascertain whether the deluge has abated. The differences are no more than one expects to find when a folklore story passes into another language and another culture. The Israelite knew nothing about the building of boats, and the story does not have a boat; it has an "ark," a floating box or house modeled on the craft of Ut-napishtim. The hero was Ziusudra in Sumerian,

John L. McKenzie

Ut-napishtim in Akkadian, and Noah in Hebrew. It is no more necessary to explain how he became Noah than it is to explain how he became Ut-napishtim. Finally the geography of the Genesis story is Mesopotamian, not Palestinian.

Naturally, the thought occurs that the deluge story is an account of a historical event preserved in Mesopotamia and in Israel. The trouble with this suggestion is that the Mesopotamian deluge is obviously not the story of a historical event; it is mythological. The Israelite story contains no element which is surely independent of the Mesopotamian story; the difference lies in the theology of the story, not in the details of the account. The suggestion that Genesis preserves the memory of a historical event through the memory of a Mesopotamian myth is so evidently contrived that it falls of its own weight. That floods occurred in Mesopotamia is obvious, but it is not to the point; the flood in the myth is cosmic not Mesopotamian.

But the Israelite writers have not preserved the Mesopotamian deluge story. They have rewritten it substantially so that it communicates an altogether different idea. In both forms of the story the actions of divine beings and the relations between the divine and the human are not accessory; they are essential to the narrative. It is not merely a story of a deluge, but rather an encounter of man with the divine. Each story is a revelation of the divine; but that which is revealed about the divine is dissimilar. The Israelite story is dependent on the Mesopotamian story; but the divine being in the Israelite story is not dependent on the Mesopotamian story. The divine being is the God of Israelite revelation, and his actions in the story are characteristic of him as he is known throughout the Old Testament. This is the specifically Israelite element in the story; and the introduction of the Israelite God has transformed the story.

An enumeration of the antitheses between the two stories in this respect will make clear what the Israelite authors accomplished. The Mesopotamian story is initiated by the decision of Enlil to destroy mankind. This decision is unmotivated. The biblical story places the motive in the wickedness of man, and the deluge becomes not an act of capricious anger but an act of judgment. In the Mesopotamian story the hero of the deluge is saved by the secret revelation of Ea, another god. Within the monotheism of the Bible no such divergence of purpose is possible; Noah is spared through the revelation of the same God who brings the flood, and he is saved because he is innocent of the wickedness which elicits the judgment. The Israelite God intends to renew mankind, not to destroy it. After the deluge there can be no dispute among the gods in the Israelite story. Where Ea charges Enlil with excessive anger, Yahweh makes a covenant by which he pledges himself that there will not be another totally destructive deluge. Noah is not rewarded with immortality, for Israelite thought knew nothing of human beings who were granted this prerogative.

Behind these differences lie divergent complexes of ideas. Neither the Mesopotamian nor the Israelite deluge stories are clear by themselves; each story illuminates the other and shows what the authors intended to do. By comparison it becomes clear that to call these "flood stories" is to miss the major theme. The stories are concerned with a much deeper problem than the flood itself; and against this problem, discussion of the historical character of the flood or of its extension can look trivial. In the ancient world the myth explored and stated problems which in the recent and modern world are discussed in philosophy and theology. The problem touched on in the Mesopotamian myth is the nature of the gods and their attitude toward mankind exhibited in the phenomena of nature. An answer to the problem is given in the myth.

Evaluating the Deluge Myth

The cosmic deluge is an example of the destructive forces of nature. The dimensions of the catastrophe exceed any known historical incident, but the principle does not depend on the number of persons involved. The problem is simply that men often die by the concurrence of natural forces, and sometimes in numbers so large that they are shocking. The Sumerians and the Babylonians did not treat this problem as one of nature; nature was the field of divine activity, all natural occurrences were the effect of the will of the gods. To the question why the gods should will the destruction of men, the deluge story shows that there is no answer. When the gods are angry, men perish; but man should not look for a rational motivation of the divine anger. The anger of the gods may be rational or it may be capricious; it makes no difference to man whether it is one or the other, for man is equally helpless in either case.

When Ea protests against the excess of Enlil, he speaks for Mesopotamian man. The Mesopotamian accepted the irrational caprice of the gods; it was a personal interpretation of phenomena which are irrational viewed personally. He had learned to live with the gods, for the same will which brought death conferred life. His happiness lay in adjusting himself to this will in all its unpredictability. But there were limits beyond which the Mesopotamian felt the gods should not go. Such were the massive disasters which sweep away human life as if it were so much rubbish. He could tolerate lesser agents such as predatory beasts, famine and disease, but when the whole of nature turned against him, he felt that the gods had passed the limits of decent anger. Does this protest have its roots in the memory of some prehistoric disaster? No doubt it does, but one need not think that the disaster was the deluge described in the story. The protest arises from man's experience of nature as hostile, and his identification of this hostility with the anger of the gods.

To the Israelite such a conception of God and nature was intolerable. The Israelites, too, experienced God in nature, and interpreted its phenomena as the effects of his will. Their idea of nature and natural forces was no more impersonal than the Mesopotamians. When nature afflicted them, they took it as an act of the anger of God. They could not attribute to the God whom they worshipped a capricious and irrational anger. If God were angry, his anger was rationally motivated and explicable. If he were angry at men, it was because men gave him cause for anger; and men do this by rebellion. Nature is the arm of God's punishment of the wicked; and in most of the Old Testament

Evaluating the Deluge Myth

this principle is followed rigorously to its conclusion. Those who are punished are wicked; the wrath of God exhibited in nature is sufficient evidence for us. If Sodom and Gomorrah are totally destroyed, it is because there is no single righteous person left after Lot and his family were led forth. An obvious corollary to this subject is the universal sickness of mankind; and this corollary the Israelites accepted.

Yet they accepted it with reservations. The idea of a God who was consumed with anger was foreign to Israelite belief. If God were angry, it was righteous anger; but righteous anger had to be tempered with mercy if it were to remain righteous. Man is wicked, but he is also weak in confrontation with God; and God takes account of his weakness. In the biblical deluge story the convenant in which God pledges not to annihilate man entirely corresponds to the speech of Ea in the Mesopotamian story. The biblical account is not a rebuke of God, as Ea rebukes Enlil; but it affirms that such total wrath is not suitable to God. God punished man in moderation, less than man deserves. Having punished totally once, he will not do it again.

This may seem to be a quite primitive theological view, and so it is; but we must consider the theological view to which it was opposed. The Israelite encountered in the

John L. McKenzie

Mesopotamian deluge story a theory of nature and the gods proposed with some imagination and vigor. The theory was congenial to Mesopotamian religion and gave man a certain satisfaction in his despair. He simply renounced any effort to find moral patterns in the behavior of the gods; and he was thus released from the compulsion to find moral patterns in his own life. The Israelite found this view expressed in myth. He did not compose a theoretical refutation; he rewrote the myth. The God who acts in the deluge story is the same God who acts throughout the Old Testament. The Israelite inserted him into the deluge story and thus showed that the Mesopotamian view was not imposed even in the thought patterns of the deluge myth. A story which originally was a statement of divine unrighteousness becomes in Israelite hands a story of divine righteousness and a vindication of the divine will that men should be righteous.

I present this as a sample of modern methods of interpretation. The first question which the interpreter asks is not, "What happened?" but, "What does this text mean?" In this instance the Mesopotamian sources of the deluge story show us the patterns of thought and the forms of literature in which the biblical writer moves. They show us the thesis his own story opposes.

Evaluating the Deluge Myth

He employs the same techniques of imagination and narrative which the Mesopotamian writers employed; he meets them on their own ground in order to arrive at an idea of God different from theirs. He shows literary dependence on the Mesopotamian writings; but he shows theological independence. The God of whom he writes is not a God of his own invention, but the God who revealed himself in Israel. The deluge story so understood makes sense in its own literary type, which is the myth; we can see what the author intended to do and the means which he used to accomplish his purpose.

The State in Christian Perspective

OSCAR Cullman once wrote that interest in the problem of church and state usually becomes vital only when open conflict between the two arises. He could have added that open conflict does not create an atmosphere favorable to clear thinking. A heated dispute is not directed to the discovery and exposition of the truth but rather to a defensive statement of convictions which are maintained all the more firmly because they are threatened. Cullman's remark had reference to the European theological discussion which was set off by the rise of National Socialism in Germany. In this discussion, as Rudolf Schnackenburg noted, Catholics took little part. If European Catholics were not engaged, American Catholics were even less concerned. There has not been a genuine church-state conflict in this country since the signing of the Constitution. Here there has been and still is an atmosphere in which scholars could think on the question without feeling a compulsion to take a defensive position. The unfinished work of John Courtney Murray is a splendid example of constructive thinking; the fact that his work is unfinished shows that the defensive attitude still exists.

Murray's work at least made it clear that there is no "Catholic" thesis on the question in the proper sense of the term. The political-ethical theses which have been maintained, and some of which have become conventional, are based on the historical acts of the church, theoreticaly justified by philosophical reasoning. There is no theological thesis of the relations of church and state; and "theological" here, like "Catholic" above, is used in the proper and rigorous sense. This is a simple statement of fact with no implications that a theological thesis cannot be reached. No thesis, either philosophical or theological, is intended here, nor any argument directed against any existing thesis. I intend a simple inquiry into what the New Testament has to say about the problem.

The inquiry is not easy, but the work done by scholars permits one to pass over some points quickly. The discussion carried on in Europe reached no consensus; the texts permit one to find in the New Testament a positive affirmation of the values of the state, a negative rejection of the state, and a neutral position. The discussion also permits one to say that the problem, if its urgency is judged by the number of texts which can be adduced as directly pertinent, is not an urgent problem in the New Testament. It permits one to say also that one must be very cautious in forming generalizations from the New Testament texts, which reflect a concrete historical situation. And here two conditions in which the New Testament texts must be considered should be mentioned.

The first condition is that the New Testament did not arise in a vacuum; here as elsewhere we look for the background of thought in which the New Testament was composed, and here as elsewhere we look at the Old Testament and Judaism. "Thought" is hardly the correct word for what we find about the state in the Old Testament, but fortunately the material can be summed up briefly. The Old Testament knows only two states: the monarchies of Israel and Judah in one group, and all other states together. Israel is submitted to God; all other states are not in submission. Other states are granted power by God; they are the rod of his anger, like Assyria (Is. 10:5), or the earth is given into their hands, like Nebuchadnezzar of Babylon (Jer. 27). When this happens, to resist them is to resist God himself. But they are unbelieving and godless, and all of them will ultimately perish in the judgments of God. The Old Testament sees no enduring society of men living in peace and order until the reign of God is firmly and finally established. Man cannot build an enduring society; the Old Testament goes immediately from historical states to the eschatological reign.

The second condition is the concrete historical situation of the New Testament. The New Testament knows nothing of "the state" in the abstract. The only state it knows is Rome; and Rome was a superstate, effectively a world state. It was very nearly as much a part of existence as the atmosphere. We cannot talk about the New Testament teaching on the state; we can talk only of the New Testament's attitude toward Rome, and we can make extended generalizations as far as our generalization corresponds to the historical reality of Rome. A synthesis of church-Rome relationships may and indeed ought to be the foundation of a synthesis of church-state relationships, but the two are not identical. This is important precisely because Rome was a world state; not only was there nothing with which to compare it, there was also no known alternative to chaos and barbarism. To this we shall return.

There are only two sayings of Jesus which have any direct reference to the state: the answer of Jesus to the question about the tribute and the answer to Pilate concerning the nature of the kingship of Jesus. The more one thinks about the words, "Render to Caesar the things that are Caesar's, and to God the things that are

God's" (Mk. 12:17; Mt. 22:21; Lk. 22:25), the more one suspects that they are not the answer to the question but a refusal to answer. Jesus cannot possibly have divided man's allegiance between God and Caesar. If God's claims are total—and nothing else is conceivable—can Caesar have any claims? The obscurity of the answer has elicited a massive literature of interpretation, none of which is satisfying. One can only conclude that God does not exact tribute, and that tribute is due to him in whose coinage the tribute is paid. Tribute was and is an acknowledgement of submission. The acceptance of a political authority does not of itself take anything away from what is due to God. The saying implies nothing about the right of the ruler to exact tribute, which is precisely the question asked; and this is why I believe that Jesus refused to answer. Instead of a *de jure* answer, he treated the question *de facto*. The fact was that the Jews were governed by Caesar and there was nothing they could do about it. If they used his money, he could get their tribute. By what means or in what quantity or by what right—these questions are not answered. We may conjecture that to Jesus they were not important. What he taught that man could be and do did not depend on Caesar. Caesar had to be accepted as a fact—like the atmosphere, as I have observed. Like the weather, he might be good or bad; but for the end which Jesus presented, he could be ignored.

The second saying of Jesus which bears on the state is his answer to Pilate's question about his kingship. Jesus affirms that he is a king, but that his kingdom is not of or from this world (Jn. 18:36-37). This is a clear disclaimer of any political involvement, and Pilate took it in this sense; whatever Pilate's skepticism about the truth, he understood at once that the case of Jesus did not fall under his jurisdiction. While this dialogue is missing in the Synoptic Gospels, they likewise tell that Pilate at first admitted no guilt in Jesus.

This is an answer and not a refusal to answer; but the answer is in line with the saying about tribute paid to Caesar. Jesus denies that the government has any reason to be concerned with him; he also denies that he has any concern with the government. No relationship is assumed or hinted; no union, no separation, no concordat—in short, no problem. Jesus and Caesar, to borrow a phrase from the text itself, move in different worlds. Neither contributes to the other; neither owes anything to the other. And this was perceived at once by an administrator who probably did not reach the level of the best men in the foreign service of Rome.

We can add a third saying of Jesus, although it does not touch the state directly. Jesus demands that his followers should not behave like those who lord it over the Gentiles and exercise authority over them; whoever is great among his followers must be the slave of all (Mk. 10:42-44; Mt. 20:25-27; Lk. 22:25-27). This saying is not hostile to the state; neither is it friendly. There will be authority and subjects in the company of the followers of Jesus; but the exercise of the authority must have no resemblance to secular government. Positively, the one who holds authority is the slave of others, but not their master. This is certainly a new conception of authority. It leaves no room in the church for anything resembling the secular government of the ancient world; this is scarcely an endorsement of secular government as a part of the Christian way of life.

In the last exchange between Jesus and Pilate which John records, Jesus says that Pilate has his power over Jesus from above (Jn. 19:11). I defer any discussion of this text until we come to Paul's text in Romans 13. For the moment we may notice that in the context of the Passion narrative and of the other sayings of Jesus, the text would never stand as a support for the divine right of Caesar. This reservation should be recalled when the text of Romans 13 is examined.

The scattered allusions to the state in the New Testament outside the Gospels are likewise few and almost entirely casual; but a pattern can be distinguished. When Paul sees Christ delivering the kingdom to the Father after destroying every rule and authority and power (I Cor. 15:24), he foresees the survival of no state in the eschatological kingdom. If marriage does not survive in the resurrection (Mk. 12:25; Mt. 22:30; Lk. 20:35), neither does the less personal and less intimate society of the state. Paul here echoes the Old Testament and Judaism, mentioned above; no human society survives the judgment of God, and the eschatological reign of God leaves no room for any merely human power. The state is clearly one of the features of "this world" which has no lasting reality.

Similarly, the transitory nature of the state is implied in Phillippians 3:20 and Hebrews 13:14. Paul assures the Philippians that their *politeuma* is in heaven. This is an extremely interesting choice of words. *Politeuma* is as near the English word *state* as any Greek word; but in usage it most frequently designates a colony of foreign residents. The implications are clear. The Christian is never identified with the state as other citizens are. From the citizens and peoples of the Roman Empire, Rome demanded supreme loyalty; and this loyalty was sanctioned by a religious motif, the cult of the divine Caesar. The supreme loyalty of the Christian was to the reign of God, present in the church and moving toward the eschatological consummation. The author of Hebrews writes in the same line of thought when he says that we have not here a lasting city but seek the one that is coming (13:14). In the Hellenistic-Roman world, the city, the Polis, was the focus of civilized living. Every man had his Polis or ought to have, without which he was homeless and rootless. The Christian, too, has his Polis which gives him home and identity; but it is the eschatological Polis of the reign of God.

Paul would not have the Christians of Corinth recur to the government even in the ordinary and useful service of the courts of law (1 Cor. 6:1-8). In a genuine Christian community, no disputes which demand a judicial decision ought to arise at all; the Christian would yield before the dispute reaches that point. But Paul is realist enough to know that disputes will arise; if they do, they should be settled out of court by agreement reached within the Christian community, and not be referred to the unrighteous and the unbeliever. The Christian transformation, Paul certainly thinks, should make laws and courts unnecessary; and what would this leave for the state to do?

It seems that the texts mentioned so far can be classified as neutral in their attitude toward the state—remembering that "the state" is always the concrete historical state of Rome. We now turn to some texts in which the attitude is clearly hostile. These texts are not numerous; they are all found in the Apocalypse. Rome is the Beast (Apoc. 13) and the Great Whore of Babylon (Apoc. 17), who will be destroyed by God's avenging judgments (Apoc. 18). As in the Old Testament, the overthrow of the world power issues in the eschatological reign of God (Apoc. 19-22). The change of tone from the other New Testament writings is evident, and the explanation of the change of tone is evident also. The Apocalypse was written after the church had experienced persecution under Nero and Domitian. Rome could no longer be simply ignored as having no relevance to the proclamation of the Gospel and the establishment of the church. It had become an enemy and subject to judgment; and the Apocalypse draws on the apocalyptic imagery of the Old Testament and Judaism to portray this judgment in vivid terms.

To arrange the texts as I have done could be considered slanting the evidence. But it may help to understand how Hans Windisch could have written that Romans 13:1-7 is a foreign body in the New Testament. This passage is in all probability the source of other passages in which the same friendly attitude toward Rome is exhibited (1 Pet. 2:13-17; 1 Tim. 2:1-2; Tit. 3:1). Here Paul proposes subjection to "the powers that be" for conscience's sake, payment of taxes, respect and honor to those to whom respect and honor are due. These recommendations do not go beyond the neutral attitude found elsewhere; but the basis on which Paul argues is novel. Obedience is due to authority because all authority is instituted by God; authority is the minister of God for the good of those who are ruled, and the agent of the wrath of God on the wrongdoer.

One feels a certain uneasiness when this passage is compared not only with the texts of the Gospel, but especially when it is compared with 1 Corinthians 6:1-8. There is no open contradiction, but there is a difference of mood and attitude. The exegetical controversies of recent years have revolved around the problem of whether Paul here gives Rome a positive value which it does not have elsewhere in the New Testament. If he does, the positive value consists in the position of Rome as an authority instituted by God and empowered to act as the minister of God's judgments "for your good." Does this establish the divine right of the state to rule?

Before one makes the affirmative answer which seems too obvious, one has to set this passage in the context of thought in which Paul lived. And the first element is the neutrality toward the state found in the sayings of Jesus. The second element is the Old Testament idea of the foreign state as the agent of God's judgments. What the prophets say of the state with reference to Israel is here said by Paul with reference to the individual criminal. The divine right of the state is no more clearly affirmed in one case than it is in the other. If one who resisted Nebuchadnezzar could be said by Jeremiah to resist God, so one who resists Rome could be said by Paul to resist God. That the power is given to Rome by God must be understood in biblical terms; and in biblical terms there is only one being possessed of power, and that is God. All power is derived from him, granted by him; but in biblical terms this does not establish the agent who receives power as either good or bad. Is Rome as the agent of God's wrath any better or worse than Assyria as the agent of God's wrath? In the wide view of biblical thought, there is no contradiction whatever between Paul's words in Romans 13 and what is written in the Apocalypse. The Beast and the Great Whore do not cease to be the minister of God's judgment; nor do they cease to be authorities instituted by God. Jesus, we have noticed, attributes to God the power which Pilate has over his life. Paul's conception of power does not differ. And here we turn up an important idea in the biblical conception of the state which is not at first apparent: the Bible never discusses what we could call the justice or the legitimacy of a government. If it exists, it is a power; and if it is a power it has received power from God, because it could not get power from any other source. To this we shall have to return.

A number of recent writers have looked for an explanation of Paul's thought in Romans 13 in the idea of the angels of the nations; this idea appears in Daniel 10:13, 20 and in the apocalyptic literature of Judaism.

These are not the conventional "angels" of Christian art and devotion; they are cosmic beings whose scope and power is, to put it delicately, ambiguous, and neither angelic nor demonic is the precise word for them. The power of the nations is mediated to them by God through these cosmic beings. Most interpreters have refused to see an allusion to this belief in Romans 13, and it is perhaps better not to lean on it too heavily, in spite of the fact that allusions to cosmic powers are sufficiently numerous in the Pauline writings. But with or without the cosmic beings, the view shows us how Paul fits the power of the state into his scheme. The state—and it is especially easy to conceive of the world state of Rome in this way—is one of the cosmic powers, a part of the structure of the material universe. Like all such powers, it is instituted by God and is his agent. Like all such powers, it can exhibit demonic traits at times. But one does not fight the state any more than one would fight the weather; and this attitude gives the state precisely that positive moral value which the weather has, no more and no less. The state is part of the condition of human existence. If the state is so conceived, Paul's words in Romans 13 fall into harmony with the words of Jesus and of Paul himself elsewhere. The state remains indifferent in the Christian way of life.

If this is the correct understanding of Romans 13—and for such a difficult passage probability is all one can invoke in one's favor—then we can synthesize New Testament thought in a form in which it does not appear in the New Testament. The controlling factor is the sayings of Jesus. His words, as I have already suggested, nearly ignore the state. There is not the slightest indication that he conceived political means for the advancement of the church. The state can neither help nor hinder the Gospel. The Christian lives in a state as he lives in a climate; neither makes any difference to his Christian profession. Whether the state is one state or another is likewise irrelevant. I use this word, which some may find too strong, because I can find nothing in the words of Jesus which tells me how to form a judgment on these matters. Render to Caesar what is his; Jesus does not tell me to examine Caesar's credentials and to measure him against an abstract standard of law and justice. And if Jesus made no distinction between a just government and an unjust government, I see four conclusions which can be drawn from his silence: (1) All governments are equally just; (2) No government is just; (3) It makes no difference whether the government is just; (4) The word "just" is meaningless when applied to government. No one of these conclusions fits into our patterns of thought. Shall we tailor the words of Jesus to fit our patterns, or shall we revise our patterns?

That the New Testament contains no theology or philosophy of the state does not imply that we should have none. The New Testament has no theory of the movement of vehicular traffic either, but we are not unfaithful to the Gospel when we devise theories. But we are better aware of the relative importance of the values we deal with; we cast no halo of religious value over right-handed rather than left-handed roadways. The New Testament, I have emphasized, is historically conditioned; it knows only Rome and not the state in the abstract. The New Testament does not touch a state which is Christian, even in the minimal sense—by which I mean that all its members are Christian. When this happens, has not a change occurred which compels Christians to go beyond the Gospel? Does the simple neutrality of the Gospel suffice for this new situation?

It has been assumed practically since the

Edict of Milan that the Gospel is not a sufficient guide for life in a Christian state; and one is surprised how easily this has been assumed. Something has been inserted between the kingdom of this world and the eschatological reign which the Bible does not put there. In a matter of such importance one should expect that biblical sources might offer some positive guidance. That they do not may of itself be illuminating; perhaps the Christian should respond to the Christian state as the primitive church responded to Rome. What can be said is that the New Testament foresees no Christian state, and that it has no specific recommendations for behavior in a Christian state.

I pass over the historical question of whether there has ever been a genuine Christian state because it is not relevant; I know that I should have no trouble finding support for the thesis that the Christian state has never existed. We can ask whether the state is an object of redemption—and this is substantially to ask whether the state can become Christian. Perhaps the question cannot be answered; but the implications of the question should not be exaggerated. Cooking, weaving, metallurgy and such activities have no place in the eschatological region; but they belong to "this age," they are a necessary part of the human condition. They become no problem unless men seek them instead of the reign of God and his righteousness—unless cooking, for instance, were regarded as the supreme human fulfillment. Paul once spoke of those whose god is their belly. In a state which practiced the Caesar cult, he could have spoken of those whose god is their state; and the author of the Apocalypse did speak of them.

The question arises because of the evident contrast between political morality and personal morality; and if there is no political morality beyond the ethics of survival, then the question cannot even arise. It is clear that the Christian must in some situations refuse survival; I do not know whether any system of political morality permits this option to the state. It seems clear also that political morality permits men to do in organized groups what Jesus said they should not do as individuals. This distinction was not made by him. The state does not do good to its enemies. It does not turn the other cheek, or walk the additional mile, or give the cloak when the tunic is demanded. It does not deny itself and take up its cross. It is solicitous about food and clothing, and would be unfaithful to its duty if it considered the lilies of the field and trusted in its heavenly Father. It defends itself by arms, apparently excepting itself from the saying of Jesus that they who take the sword perish by the sword. I have already noticed that Paul sees no room for law and courts in a Christian community. The state becomes an impersonal and therefore an amoral entity; but can it ever become really impersonal?

It can be argued, of course, that the state provides for the citizens necessary services and protection which they are unable to secure as individuals; and that therefore its morality cannot be the morality of the individual man. The Christian ideal can and should be practiced by the Christian in his personal relations; it cannot be practiced in his political relations. This position has some validity; but it can be asked to what extent the citizen enjoys the freedom to live the purely personal relations. In how many of his actions is he the political animal and not the Christian free of political obligations? An examination of this problem might disclose that the Christian has very little free room left to live according to Christian charity. The influence of the state is far more extensive than its power, even in what are called free democratic societies. It is magnificent testimonial to the moral integrity of the United States of America that with the exception of Vietnam it has presented to its Christian citizens no moral problem of sufficient magnitude and complexity to warrant a serious theological discussion. One wonders whether such unblemished probity could be found even in the government of the Catholic Church.

If this be thought cynical—and it will be—let us consider the alternative. The alternative is that the actions of the government are not subject to the moral judgment of the individual citizen. Our morality of the state can be reduced to the simple and single obligation of obeying the state, because the state is the supreme judge of what it must do in order to fulfill its duty. And if this be the basic principle of political morality, it becomes easier to understand why the New Testament does not distinguish between a just and an unjust government. No one of us wants to put our own government on what we think is the moral level of Señor Castro's; but both governments are dedicated to their own end, which is survival. If Jesus were asked the question about tribute in Cuba, would his answer be different from what it was in Judaea—or what it would be in the United States? Then and now the citizen must obey the state because only the government has the information on which its decisions are based.

I do not wish to affirm or even to imply that the state has become the supreme arbiter of morality on the political life of the citizen; but I have no hesitation in affirming that it has happened before. Have I any reason to doubt that it can happen in any state? Is there something demonic in the very constitution of the state which drives it ultimately to play God in determining the moral life of its citizens? And will not a Christian state do this perhaps more quickly than a secular state, given the tendency of Christians to be assured that God is on the side of their good conscience? The history of the church united with the Christian state is too largely a history of Caesaropapism.

If the state cannot survive except as a secular amoral entity, one can see why the attitude of the New Testament is neutral. If the state arrogates to itself the right to make supreme moral judgments, it becomes the Beast of the Apocalypse. The New Testament does not recommend rebellion in such cases; it recommends martyrdom and nothing else. The state will endure until God's judgment strikes it; while it endures, the Christian in such a state has no choice except to hold to his loyalty to the reign of God—to which the secular state will transfer him. But even in these exceptional crises, the state remains a part, and a necessary part, of the human condition.

The human condition is the condition of fallen and sinful man. From this condition the state cannot redeem him. It is a part of the human condition as death, concupiscence and nature are a part. Man cannot escape the state; he has to live in a political society. There is no virtue in

The State of Christian Perspective

living in a political society any more than there is virtue in being mortal. It is one of the things which man must endure because he lives under a curse. In the reign of God he will be redeemed from this as from other elements of the curse. His redemption is achieved in and through the human condition, of which the state is a part.

These questions, considerations and doubts may suggest an excessive otherworldliness. They may be taken to imply a flight from social responsibility and the construction of a Christian ghetto neither influencing nor influenced by the political life of man. If they are so taken, the same interpretation could be placed on observations that the state of the Christian is heaven and that the Christian has no enduring city here; and I did not write these observations. One who lives the Christian life described in the Gospels will fairly surely fulfill his social responsibilities. Jesus told his disciples to love their enemies; he did not tell them to be good citizens, but if they love their enemies the recommendation of good citizenship is superfluous.

No, the Christian must live in the state, and he must live in it as a Christian. His Christian life is the only security the state has against becoming the Beast and the Great Whore. As long as a sufficient number of citizens insist that the state remain within its limits, it will do its duty and be less of an obstacle to the establishment of the reign of God. The state which knows that its citizens will refuse it a total commitment will find it difficult to institute modern versions of the Caesar cult. The state whose citizens will not permit it to attempt what it cannot do may more surely accomplish the things it can do. But here we risk building a Utopia. The neutrality of the Gospels is an extremely realistic attitude. If you ask the New Testament what the state can accomplish, the answer is: nothing. Whether it is better or worse, it cannot construct a lasting city. The Christian deals with his state as he deals with his food, his clothing and his house. Like them, it is necessary. Like them, it is used up, it is consumed, it wears out. Like them, it can become a preoccupation which excludes any other interest. The New Testament has no philosophy of the state and no political ethics because Rome, viewed in the light of the Gospels, was essentially trivial.

The Bible: A Progress Report

IN order to understand the present position of biblical studies in the church, it is necessary to go back almost to the beginning of the twentieth century. The present position of biblical studies is the fruit of development which was long and at times rather complex. The movement known as modernism which arose at the beginning of this century and was vigorously suppressed by the Holy See between 1900 and 1910 was deeply concerned with biblical studies. All biblical scholars, not only those who are called modernists, felt that Roman Catholic biblical studies had long been at a standstill in contrast to biblical studies in the Protestant churches, which at that time seemed to have reached a peak of vigorous and creative interpretation. New insights seemed to arise almost every year. These insights worried conventional Catholic theologians, who as a group felt that biblical interpretation threatened some of their cherished positions. In fact, these insights did threaten their positions but they were not as dangerous as these theologians feared.

In any case, they made their concern known to

the Roman authorities and within the space of about ten years modernism as a theological movement in the Catholic Church simply came to an end. Biblical studies also came to an end. There was practically no progress in Catholic biblical studies between the years, let us say, 1905 and 1940. But what was done was done by a very few scholars who did it with more caution than they would have used had they been left to their own judgment. Consequently, Roman Catholic biblical studies, which were already out of date in 1890, had gone no farther in 1935.

This meant effectively that in the Catholic Church the Bible and biblical studies had almost no influence on popular piety, on education, on preaching, and on any of those ways in which the church communicates its message to its members. Before the beginning of the Second World War there had arisen cautious but growing freedom in Catholic biblical scholars who were probably the only members of the church to recognize how far their own work was behind the work of non-Catholic scholars.

By a process which we scarcely trace, this growing freedom found expression in the pontifical document produced by Pius XII in 1943. This document, known by its Latin title. *Divino Afflante Spiritu*, set forth a program of biblical studies which, to contemporary scholars, was revolutionary in the freedom which it encouraged. And Catholic scholars were not slow to make use of this new freedom. The amount of publications concerning the Bible, the place of the Bible in education, and popular presentations other than books and magazine articles grew enormously at the conclusion of the Second World War. Many Catholics felt that they were reading the Bible for the first time. In fact, many of them were. The meaning of the Bible for Catholic belief and Catholic life had a depth and richness which they had never known or suspected.

The place of biblical studies in the movement which led to the Second Vatican Council is difficult to assess. Some observers called the Second Vatican Council the product of the new theology, which designates the theology current in the church between the Second World War and the beginning of the Council itself. Others would reverse the image and say that the Vatican Council produced the new theology. My own personal opinion is that the Second Vatican Council has rather indicated something of a halt in theological progress and that as far as one can make such judgments, the Vatican Council was an attempt to sum up the new theology, an attempt which was so successful that the new theology has done very little since the end of the Council.

In any case, what were called the new biblical

studies were highly important in producing the theology and the intellectual atmosphere which brought about the Second Vatican Council as an expression of Roman Catholic belief. No one would deny the importance of biblical work in this and it seems idle to attempt to compare its importance to other branches of theology. It is both more important and more interesting to attempt some evaluation of the role of biblical studies in church renewal rather than merely in the Second Vatican Council. The brief attempt which I shall make will, I hope, avoid exaggerations in either direction. I shall certainly not try to underplay the role of biblical studies, nor do I wish to overstate them. But some themes of church renewal, most of which have been expressly stated by the Vatican Council, can be called basic biblical themes. And these themes have become common, not only in writing and preaching, but also in the conversation of Catholics.

The first of these themes I would call the church as community. Older Catholics, at least, are aware that the church has not always been in their mind a community in the same sense in which a family or even a civic society is a community. The parish was often synonymous with the neighborhood which is one form of community. Yet the identity was by no means perfect. And to speak of the church as a community of love would be to most people a rather meaningless exaggeration of the religious organization to which they gave their belief and their obedience. They simply did not feel that close to their fellow Catholics. If love existed between people it arose from some other motive than community of faith.

Now the Second Vatican Council has incorporated this understanding of the church in its Acts and it has become a part of normal preaching. As to the effect of this view of the church, it is too early to assess precisely what effect it has had. How has it altered the view of Catholics toward their fellow members? I think that I detect changes in the popular mind but I am, if anything, over-sympathetic to biblical studies. I believe this is a much more healthy view, that only as a community of love does the church seem to be unique in human society. Its other features by which it binds its members it shares with the political or even the economic community. But there is only one community of love that has ever been proposed, and that is the church which we believe was founded by Jesus precisely as such a community. Anything else in the way of organization must be built upon this community of love or it simply is not the church. It is something else. The church, indeed, does have resemblances with the state and even with the business corporation and to some degree, such resemblances probably cannot be avoided. But if this is *all* the organization it has, it does not have the organization which we find in the New Testament.

The second of these themes I call the church as pilgrim people. This again is a phrase of the Second Vatican Council. It is based on a long tradition in biblical literature, going back indeed to the Old Testament. The original pilgrim people of the Bible were the Israelites finding their way from Egypt to the Promised Land. This is the image which is now presented to us Catholics as the mirror of our church here on earth.

We all learn, if we are old enough, that there are, so to speak, three churches, which the catechism described as the Church Militant, the Church Suffering, and the Church Triumphant. The Church Militant is the church of those living on earth. The Church Triumphant is those who have finished the course and have kept the faith. And the Church Suffering is those who have finished the course but have not finished it perfectly. Where does the Pilgrim People stand in this three-fold scheme? Naturally it is identical with the Church Militant. No one, I think now, would question that the word "militant" applied to the church is an unhappy designation which we are better off without; and

The Bible: A Progress Report

if we think of it as the Pilgrim People rather than the Church Militant we shall be less inclined to think of the faith as a form of combat with adversaries. The Pilgrim People are led by God. They are not pursuing any human objective. The Israelites in the desert were led by God to a place which they knew only vaguely, which they were unable to reach by themselves, and which they could reach only by submitting themselves totally to divine leadership. They have not arrived at their objective. They are on the way. They are, therefore to this degree, not perfect. They have a way to go and they have things to do. The Pilgrim People of the Old Testament are described in many passages as murmuring and rebellious. This is equally applicable to the Pilgrim People of the New Testament.

This theme, the Pilgrim People, stands in opposition to that attitude which was described during the Council by a newly coined word, triumphalism. This was the attitude that the church had attained its objectives, that it had reached perfection, that it had no place to go and really nothing else to do. It had no task except to be its own perfect self. The theme of the Pilgrim People is an express renunciation of the triumphal attitude or of the belief that the church is so perfect that it cannot grow. Naturally, the other side of this is the question of whether the Pilgrim People exhibits faults and whether its members are entitled to point them out.

This is generally, if somewhat grudgingly, recognized as a legitimate function of the members of the church. Whether the Pilgrim People is a people which confesses its sins is an implication of this theme, not yet perhaps as clear as it ought to be. If one thinks of the church as perfect and has having reached that objective which God has set for it, one effectively denies that the church can do wrong. That this is the attitude of many of its members needs no comment. Whether this attitude can be combined with the belief that the church is a Pilgrim People is indeed a difficult question. Many Catholics have long felt that to point out any fault in the church is either to tell an untruth or to wash its dirty linen in public, to use a popular metaphor. One should do neither. The answer by many wits to this position has been that it is better to wash one's linen in public than not to wash it at all, which, in the past history of the triumphal church has often been what happened. Nevertheless, the church as assembled in the Vatican Council came closer to confessing sins of the church than any of the previous twenty Councils. And it is likely that this will grow in the future, in spite of the opposition of many influential people to any sort of confession of sin on the part of the church.

The third theme I call the church as ecumenical, using a word which is not apt but the attitude which I am thinking of really has no single word to describe it. If we go back to the New Testament we find that the Gospel is addressed to all men. The proclamation of the Gospel to all men is expressly attributed to Jesus himself, more than once, although biblical scholars now believe that the church was somewhat slow in becoming aware of its universal mission. In any case, it was well aware of it before the New Testament was written because the New Testament itself witnesses to this general appeal to all men. This is the basic ecumenical quality of the church: that no one antecedently is excluded from its membership; that no human qualification is required for baptism and for faith. Paul dealt with Jewish Christians who believed that Judaism was a qualification for Christianity and Paul's great discovery was that it was not and could not be a condition, that to lay any condition down for membership in the church was to falsify the Gospel. That Paul had his problems in convincing his fellow Christians of this is evident, although the history is not as full as we should like to have it. But the attitude that some qualification is necessary for Christianity has endured long after Jewish Christians ceased to exist. It exists in the contemporary church. There is a feeling which has really never been articulated that in order to be a Catholic you really must be a member of the civilized European community and its derivatives and that if you are not a member of this community, you really cannot be a genuine and full member of the church unless you first become civilized.

We really have no Gospel to proclaim to those who are not Europeans. In the great age of discovery when the church moved into Asia, Africa and the Americas it had no place for the natives of these countries except the place held by peasants and the poor workers in Europe. It was not possible for them, the natives, to rise above that level any more than it was possible for them to become bishops. That important position had to be held by a civilized European. Most of the clergy likewise were not native. It is only in the twentieth century that we have begun to move away from this colonial kind of Catholicism in other continents and the movement has been slow, and sometimes has been accomplished over quite bitter opposition.

So far I have not spoken of ecumenism in the sense in which the word is usually intended, that is, of the position of the Catholic church in the face of the Protestant churches. I say, in the face of, because I do not wish to say in opposition to. When the Reformation happened and for the centuries which followed, I think it is no exaggeration to say that the Roman Catholic Church dealt with the Protestant churches in much the same way as it dealt with the Moslems or the Jews. Now that kind of controversy is no longer carried on. Naturally the Protestants responded in kind when they were treated as unbelievers and the bitter tone of early controversy is something which no one regrets losing. We do not need that. We cannot use it. We recognize and the Vatican Council expressly recognized that the Protestant churches are Christians. They are fellow Christians with Catholics. The theology of a large Christian community, however, has not yet been formed, either by Catholics or by Protestants. There seems to be no reason why it could not be and I myself am convinced that it can happen, that it must happen, that it is essential to the survival of Christianity, that such an awareness of a Christian community is a theological task that will be accomplished. If it is not, then the Christian church will cease to exist. I do not believe that is going to happen and for that reason I am convinced that the Church will do what it must do to survive.

At the present, I must confess the signs of this task being done are not impressive. The attitude of Catholics and Protestants toward each other of course has changed tremendously in two or three generations. This is generally thought to be a healthy development, even though there is some danger of a rather bland Christianity which really affirms very little and demands very little from its members. We must, I believe, here have some confidence in the Holy Spirit that it will not tolerate such blandness, that we must after all leave something for the Holy Spirit to do. And I assume that since the churchmen themselves do not seem to be taking very good care of this, that I can, at the moment, trust no one but the Holy Spirit. No one else appears who deserves the trust.

The form of such a Christian community which would include all who are Christians, since it has no theological base, cannot be described. I have no way of anticipating what a truly Catholic church would look like, except I believe it would not look like the Roman Catholic Church. Some of my fellow Catholics will probably say that this itself is a denial that the Roman Catholic Church is the true church. I do not mean to deny it. At the same time I am aware that the Roman Catholic Church has exhibited for centuries a kind of narrowness for which I find no warrant in the Gospel. We have added demands for membership in the church that cannot be found in the New Testament. This is not to say, by the way, that they are not legitimate. The church must grow; but each such demand, each such qualification for membership, it seems, ought to be examined very, very carefully before it is imposed. And such cautious and thorough examination simply has not been made. After all, the Gospel historically was proposed in such a way that it could be grasped by any uneducated, uncivilized person who has the mental age of about eight to twelve years. To impose other things which presuppose a more advanced state of culture is to propose something that is not Christianity, although it may be quite good. But it should not be introduced into the examination for Baptism.

The fourth theme I call Authority as Service. This likewise is a theme mentioned by the Vatican Council. The paradox of the phrase is, I think, fairly obvious. But it is a surely biblical paradox. The words of Jesus quoted in the Gospels, that he who would be first among you should be the slave of others, are a first expression of this paradox. Naturally, authority in the church has come in for considerable criticism because of its failure historically to conduct itself as a servant. But in the present generation this principle that authority must serve is generally recognized. Hardly anyone now would dare to deny it expressly, although it is only a few years since some did. What form will the service take? Jesus used a metaphor. The slave—that is the word he used—is a person who has no will of his own. He is entirely for the owner. This is a social system which modern society rejects but we can understand what it means. And so, transferred to authority in the church, it means that authority has no life of its own, no purpose of its own, no objective which is of any importance. The authority in the church belongs to the members. It is their needs, their desires, even, which govern authority and this inverts the ordinary structure of political authority which Jesus expressly said in the same passage was not to be the model of authority in his church.

This attitude can now be seen in many church officers, both in their words and in their actions, in their way of handling the business of the church. The feeling that the members of the church should have a part in the work of authority through parish and diocesan councils is again the theme of the Second Vatican Council. This enables the authority to serve its members better by knowing what its members think and what its members wish. The ideal is a decision which is shared by all and as far as is possible represents a genuine consensus. In human affairs perfect consensus is hardly possible and it should not be here an ideal which is renounced because it is theoretically impossible. Certainly absolute authority never achieved consensus either. It simply suppressed dissent. This is not the same thing. I would say also that authority as service must be authority as a work of love primarily. If it is indeed to be a Christian authority this must be what makes it different from secular authority, that those in authority love those whom they govern and deal with them on these terms. In political society we do not expect this of our government and we do not get it. So we are not disappointed if it fails to render it. If a church authority shows itself as unloving, as impersonal, or as even hostile to those whom it governs, it fails to this degree to be authentically Christian and authentically churchly.

The fifth and last of the themes I name is the theme of Freedom in the Church. This is a somewhat ambiguous expression. Freedom depends really on who defines it. What is freedom? In a purely practical definition one may say that my freedom ends where someone else's freedom begins. But this purely theoretical statement does not settle very many practical disputes. And one function of authority is not so much to preserve itself as to preserve a freedom of all within its community: not to infringe on their freedom itself nor to allow the members to hamper the freedom of each other.

In practical ways this movement of freedom

again has shown itself in recent action. Again, no one regrets the disappearance of the famous index of forbidden books. We may simply bury it quietly and here notice only that it was a form of inhibition of freedom which should never have been employed in the first place. If it is wrong now it was wrong in the sixteenth century. We have in the Vatican Council an express declaration of the freedom of those who are in academic work to pursue their studies without hindrance. Naturally these studies are of interest to others. But interest in the work of scholars is one thing. Attempt to direct it by those who are not engaged professionally in scholarship is another. And the history of such interference with scholarship has been totally bad. It has never done any good and should, I think, be renounced in theory and in practice.

As far as the members of the church who are not scholars, who are not priests, who are, we might say, working Christians, what does freedom mean to them? We still, it seems to me, have some distance to go in convincing Catholics of their freedom of moral decisions. The theological system of recent Catholicism, insofar as it touches moral conduct, has been compared to the Jewish interpretation of the law. It sometimes appeared to be an attempt to have a prefabricated law decision for every possible situation into which the Catholic, cleric or lay, might

The Bible: A Progress Report

fall. Theology was very slow to tell a Catholic that this is a moral decision which he and only he could make. It is not always a clear question of what is right and what is wrong. Karl Rahner once said that the most important decisions in any person's life are moral and that for these important decisions, there is no book. He instances, for example, the decision to marry or not to marry, or to marry this one rather than that. These, he said, are moral decisions, they are highly important decisions, and no one can make them except the person who is doing the marrying. This can be extended to other moral situations, as well. We cannot give that kind of direction which the scribes of the New Testament attempted to give the Jewish community. And in this sense we now recognize, I believe, that freedom does not mean anything unless it means the freedom to make one's own mistakes, rather than have others' mistakes imposed upon one.

If these are some of the results of biblical studies in church renewal, I think that we would admit that it is an impressive list. I think also that my colleagues in theology would be ready to say that biblical studies at least were deeply concerned in the preparation of these themes, although they should not be given all the credit that there is. But the fact that these are some of the important results of biblical studies and not necessarily all the results of them leads to the question, why have biblical studies apparently stalled? What has happened?

I think some reasons can be given for this lag, this change, but in the long run, it escapes explanation. There are certain changes in style, in thought, in customs, which historians observe and are often unable to explain. Changes in the ways of thinking or in artistic taste are not quite as irrational as change of styles of clothing sometimes appear to be. But at the same time, there are certain popular movements which lie too far beneath the surface for the historians or the journalist to understand them. With these reservations, I shall attempt some explanation of at least why biblical studies, so short a time ago so active, now seem to be almost inactive.

The first and most obvious factor is that biblical studies in the Catholic Church attempted to make up a great deal of time since 1943. I said earlier that biblical studies which were out of date in 1890 had hardly advanced by 1943. I say hardly; there were advances. Since that time, one simply realizes that biblical studies moved too far, too fast, too soon. Some Protestant colleagues have observed that in the Catholic Church biblical studies did in the space of 25 years what in the Protestant churches took 100. This accelerated, even feverish, pace of progress could not possibly have endured. We moved rapidly because we were far behind. We are no longer far behind and the rapid pace simply is now the normal pace, it seems, of biblical scholarship.

This does not mean that biblical studies have ended but that the thrill which was involved in the pace of the last 30 years is no longer there. And the public, therefore, which was somewhat fascinated by the rapid pace of the progress is less fascinated by the slower and surer progress of scholarship which is normal. This at least is a factor that has to be considered. We slowed up because we had to. And anyone who has traveled in a jet plane realizes that the reduction of speed from 600 to 300 miles an hour seems to the terrified traveler to be almost a complete stall. It is not: 300 miles an hour is still pretty good progress and so I think biblical studies are making good progress but half as fast or even less.

I do not believe that repression by church authority is any factor in this. I mentioned one of the fruits of church renewal as freedom. Biblical studies in the church have certainly benefited from this atmosphere of freedom as much as anyone else and possibly more than anyone else. Biblical scholars are likely to think this because they, if they are old enough, are conscious of the repression that their discipline once felt. And once that is removed, one feels almost total freedom. In fact, no biblical scholar has been troubled by church authority since the second world war and with past history of biblical studies, this is remarkable. We have been free. If we are not doing our work now it is not because anyone is placing obstacles in the way.

I think, however, that there has been in recent years a lack of interest in biblical studies. One can see this, for instance, in the way in which biblical studies now attract young men. They do not attract as many as they did 20 years ago. Then it was obvious that there was much to be done and the chance to engage in something which was worthwhile and exciting. That is not so obvious at the present moment. And, therefore, the number of young men or young women that now take up biblical studies professionally is sharply reduced. The whole area of theology has felt this depression, by the way. It is not simply biblical studies. The stall of which I have spoken is not confined to the biblical area in theology; it has affected other areas as well.

One may also cite the absence in recent years of what we will call exciting developments. I am thinking, for instance, of such men as Rudolph Bultmann, who hardly expected, when he was a young professor in Germany, to become a household word in North America. By one of those inexplicable tricks of genius or of destiny, he uttered in 1941, the year in which German lecturers did not get wide circulation, a phrase "demythologizing the New Testament" which ultimately became known to practically every member of the Christian church throughout the world. Bultmann was much more vilified than understood. His thesis was that we must proclaim the Gospel to the modern man in terms which attract him and which he can understand. And Bultmann felt that part of the obstacle of the Gospel for modern man was the antiquated worldview which the Bible contains. Whether this is true or not may be open to question. The general statement that the Gospel is usually *not* proclaimed to modern man in terms which excite his interest, which speak to his concern, that thesis is incontestable, and because of Bultmann, the Christian churches have been more conscious of their failure to speak to modern man in language which he is willing to hear. This is an example of an exciting development.

Such an exciting development has not happened really since Bultmann. There have been minor developments, exciting but not to that degree. But at the moment, the excitement is just not present in biblical studies, though one cannot predict, of course, that it will remain quiet nor can one predict an exciting development. But if anyone asks why there is a certain lag in interest, obviously this has to be brought to mind. It is now over thirty years since Bultmann's celebrated lecture and we are still talking about it, but not nearly as much as we were ten years ago. And nothing else of a comparable excitement has come up.

With these things in mind then, we still, as I said, have not quite explained why biblical studies have sort of settled down. Is there a mass fatigue among the scholars? Possibly. Some observers have said that the entire church exhibits traces of mass fatigue after the Vatican Council. We are runners who are now sitting by the roadside drawing deep breaths. Hopefully we will get up and run some more but at the moment we are not able to. Others speak of consolidating the gains of the Second Vatican Council. Frankly the gains are not that spectacular that we need to spend all this time consolidating them. Whatever it is, there is a feeling of, I call it, fatigue. And I do not believe, as I say, that one can really analyze this. What will change it is no doubt some exciting development which there is no reason to think is impossible. However, it cannot be predicted.

Our final consideration must be the task which still lies before biblical studies. And here I have already said I can predict no exciting developments, although when I consider the tasks which we must consider, there is no reason to believe that exciting developments may not be ahead of us. What is needed is not merely the possibilities but also the exciting persons to realize them. We can begin by observing that there must always be contemporary reinterpretation of the Bible. We cannot prepare a package of research which will be valid for all times and for all places. This was the ideal, I believe, of many of our predecessors in theology, to produce statements of belief which would be beyond alteration or qualification. We now know that this cannot be done. To this extent, at least, we have all become modernists. The eternal formula of belief is not something which we seek. I do not mean we expect to have a Council produce a statement to the effect that Jesus is not the Son of God, but we can never hope to make the statement that Jesus is the Son of God with that understanding which we believe is a part of the eschatological hope. It is a truth which can always be more deeply understood. And the growth in theology and growth in faith mean growth in understanding what we believe.

Now the degree to which we understand it is to a large extent conditioned by the culture in which we live. We live in probably the most sophisticated civilization which man has yet devised, so sophisticated that some are wondering whether the civilization may be a collective death wish. But in any case, we ask questions which could not have been asked in the fourth and fifth century nor in the sixteenth. And it is not possible to tell modern educated man that these are questions which he must be a good little boy and not ask. This simply removes him from the audience. He believes that he has a good mind, that it is well trained, that questions arise because it is a good, well-trained mind, and that at least if no answer is possible, that such a statement should be made only after investigation. If we fail, that we can accept. But we cannot accept refusing the effort. Man does not fear to search into mystery, as one of the biblical wise men warned him. That attitude of ancient wisdom is not found in modern wisdom; and man, who has found a way to travel to the moon, is not so easily frightened of mystery as his predecessors of two to three thousand years ago.

Now the church, of course, can be silent before such questions, in which case again, it simply doesn't speak to the concerns of modern man. Bultmann's criticism of the New Testament mythology, I have said, is open to objection. It was valid mythology in New Testament times. They were incapable of scientific understanding of the universe; and this was a statement of the human condition which was the best that men could do. I am not speaking now of the New Testament mythology. There is none such, really; it is rather the acceptance by the New Testament writers of the thought patterns of the world in which they lived. Modern man has different thought patterns. He need not rewrite the New Testament. But those who proclaim the New Testament must recognize that thought patterns are different. It is not valid, or I should say, it not vital, that the New Testament seems to believe in what Bultmann called a three-decker universe, like a club sandwich. We no longer think of the universe in those terms. And we believe basically that it is an inaccurate view of the universe.

But that is not the point. The question whether the universe is three-decker, whether it is round, whether it is square, whether it is a polygon, is not important. Whatever shape it is, the New Testament's query is, how is it related to God? And man's position in the universe is a position in the universe as God's creature, not precisely determined by how large or how small the universe is. His position before God is not altered by the larger universe which we know. But we cannot, of course, talk to modern man about heaven and hell as anything else but images of realities which are not experienced. In that sense we, too, use mythology and Bultmann's mistake was largely to believe that modern man had escaped mythology. No, he has not escaped it, he simply has created different myths and those who proclaim the Gospel must know this. A myth is, by definition, neither true nor false. Like a philosophy, it can be either. But it is an attempt to interpret man's place in the universe which reflects, as I have said, the culture in which it is produced. As the culture advances, the myth is antiquated.

This may be, indeed, the major task of biblical interpretation, and, indeed, of theology at the present time, to produce a theology which does speak to our contemporaries. We are not now attempting to produce those eternal verities. We know it is impossible. The best we can do is to speak to someone in terms which command his attention. And to that degree, the language of theology is always determined by other factors than theology. We come into a language which is ready made. It was not produced by us and we must adhere to its rules. Otherwise people simply do not hear us. Now, one observes that in the modern church there have been and still are a number of failures to heed the Bible and to apply it to life. I do not believe we need to en-numerate all of these. In the first place, we no longer have the space for that, and we would risk being offensive. But many, many Catholics have remarked the massive silence of the church before some contemporary concerns.

I am thinking, in the first place, of course, of war and peace. Now it is quite possible to speak

The Bible: A Progress Report

from the Bible to war and peace but I know no way in which what the Bible tells us about war and peace can be presented to modern governments in an acceptable form. Our temptation then has been since we know people will not accept it, therefore don't say it.

Now there is no doubt that this principle of prudence has a certain validity. But it is a very dangerous principle. In the case of war and peace, it has meant that the church has lived to a fair degree of contentment with warfare ever since Constantine. We have tried to produce a form of Christianity which will be tolerable to those who believe that the best way to deal with your enemies is not to love them but to beat their heads in. And we have done this. We have produced the ethic of the just war. This is not the New Testament and every theologian knows it. But the implication that Jesus spent his time producing impractical ideals of moral conduct has other implications which I for one would prefer not to have explored because it is effectively going to lead to a denial of Christianity as a valid system of human life.

There are other such concerns. As I say, we do not want to ennumerate them here. But about several of them, this generality, I think, can be stated. Where the church might speak, where theologians know that the church has something to say, it has surrendered the issues to others:

either to radicals or to conservatives, of which the church should be neither, and they have run away with the issues, as for instance, they did in this country with the issue of war and peace. The fact that the church was so loudly silent, permitted an exaggerated status of the ideal of peace which is not palatable even to many of us who call ourselves pacifists. The peace which I heard from radical friends was not a peace which leads to love. It is a peace which leads to hatred. And the paradox of those who proclaim peace and hatred at the same time is equally distasteful as the paradox of those who proclaim the Gosepl and the ethics of the just war at the same time.

Neither is faithful to the trust of the Gospel which is to bring men together in love. I have read statements of the advocates of peace which I find completely unChristian. And they do this because the church failed to speak its own message. This is in the instances which I mentioned surrender to the radical wing. But the church surrenders other issues to other political views which are again equally unpalatable. I am thinking now of the issue of poverty. Now, if the New Testament is clear on anything, it is clear on poverty. It is so clear that we would prefer not to hear it. Here again we have the radical approach and the conservative approach, neither of which represent the belief and the teaching of Jesus. But what has the church said in response to these exaggerated extremes? It has been very quiet, really. The attitude of the church for centuries about poverty has been this: Jesus said, Blest are you poor. And we are Christians and we will have poor people. We will have professional poor people. They will be members of religious orders. And as long as some of us are poor, we are faithful to Jesus. The poverty of religious enables the rest of the Christians to look for every dollar that they can get. And that is not really the meaning of the religious vocation or what is called evangelical poverty.

I do not know how to explain any practical implementation of the teaching of Jesus on poverty. In a certain sense, it has never been tried, as Chesterton once said about the whole of Christianity. But I can recognize that neither the radical nor the conservative approach to the problem of poverty in modern times is the Gospel, whatever it is. And since it seems to be a social problem of which the Gospel speaks, I think it would deserve the trouble of investigation, and this means theological investigation with reference to the contemporary world. The world in which Jesus lived was a different economic world from ours and his teaching on poverty can easily be called out of date because it is not relevant to our economic system. Some have called it that. Yet what is relevant? We do not seem to have dealt with the problem with any degree of success by other means which are more secular. The church has not yet found its message on this controversial topic, it seems to me, and this is certainly a part of the task of theology.

Other problems could be listed also, but as I have said, space does not permit. But the task is there, it is manifold and it touches a great many areas, not just the two on which I have chosen to dwell. These are examples of areas where the church has yielded its own mission to, say, political or social systems and has apparently decided that there are some problems which are genuine problems but which are beyond our reach. That is, of course, a denial of the power of the Gospel effectively or a plea that we have the right thing to say but it is not the right time to say it. Naturally that generally means that there never is the right time to say it and that the church lies down tranquilly as it has done so often in the past with some establishment. And when it lives at peace with the establishment, it believes that it has created a Christian community. This is the one thing possibly which the church has never yet created.